DIANA: HER NEW LIFE
by Andrew Morton

"The book said Diana would divorce Charles within the year and receive a $24.5 million settlement. . . ."
—Dan Ehrlich and Larry Sutton, *The Daily News* (New York)

" 'I'm coming back with a vengeance,' Diana is quoted as telling friends. . . . She has also admitted . . . that she views the palace, most family members and their courtiers as a 'leper colony.' "
—*New York Newsday*

"Morton started the Royal media frenzy two years ago, when he wrote *Diana: Her True Story*, which revealed the princess had attempted to commit suicide several times because she was so unhappy. Morton is closely linked to Diana's circle, and his new book is believed to be well sourced. In London, it is widely seen as Diana's reply to Charles's just-released authorized biography, in which he revealed he never loved Diana. . . . According to Morton's book, the terms of the divorce settlement have already been agreed upon by Diana's lawyers and Buckingham Palace. . . . It also says the princess was so desperate after her marriage crumbled, she threatened to run away to Australia with her two sons, William and Harry. . . ."
—Bill Hoffmann, *New York Post*

By the same author

Inside Kensington Palace
Duchess
The Wealth of the Windsors
Diana's Diary
Inside Buckingham Palace
Diana, Her True Story

DIANA

Her New Life

ANDREW MORTON

POCKET STAR BOOKS

New York London Toronto Sydney Tokyo Singapore

A Pocket Star Book published by
POCKET BOOKS, a division of Simon & Schuster Inc.
1230 Avenue of the Americas, New York, NY 10020

Copyright © 1994, 1995 by Andrew Morton
Appendix Copyright © 1994 by Wedlake Bell

First published in Great Britain by Michael O'Mara Books Limited

ISBN: 0-671-53398-3

First Pocket Books printing September 1995

10 9 8 7 6 5 4 3 2

POCKET STAR BOOKS and colophon are registered trademarks of Simon & Schuster Inc.

Cover photo by AP/Wide World

Printed in the U.S.A.

Contents

DIANA
Her New Life

Preface

THE PUBLICATION OF *Diana, Her True Story* made headlines around the world and the book became an international best-seller. Its success was due not only to the popularity of the subject, but also because it squared the editorial circle, giving detailed revelations about the royal family from named sources who were demonstrably close to the Princess of Wales.

While this enabled the book's claims to withstand a furious assault from the British Establishment and media, it meant that those who contributed found themselves as the honourable victims of a witch-hunt, their own integrity and lives under constant and often unpleasant scrutiny for no reason other than that they had had the courage to tell the truth about Diana's unhappy life inside the royal family.

1

Since then the royal caravan has moved on. The book's revelations, initially treated with scorn and scepticism, are now accepted. The evident rivalry between the Prince and Princess of Wales and the attempts by Buckingham Palace to restore the tarnished image of the House of Windsor have meant that many more people from inside the royal circle are prepared to talk frankly and freely about the reality of the modern monarchy.

That candour is tempered by an awareness of the consequences of going public: the endless phone calls, the sneering articles and the early-morning knock on the front door. As a result, while researching *Diana, Her New Life* the decision was made from the beginning that no one would be quoted by name and, furthermore, anyone who was approached by the media would deny involvement. While unsourced quotations may expose the authority of the book to question, this does not lessen its accuracy; it is the price that unfortunately has to be paid. My heartfelt thanks then to all those who collaborated in the research for *Diana, Her New Life*. It would not have been possible without the help of some old friends—and new ones. As ever, thanks to my publisher, Michael O'Mara, for his shrewd judgment, and my wife, Lynne, for her composure under often trying circumstances.

ANDREW MORTON
September 1994

2

1

The Prisoner of Wales

WHAT IS A PRINCESS FOR? Or, more accurately, what is the point of a disaffected, semi-detached Princess of Wales? A woman who often sees herself as 'the biggest prostitute in the world', who ironically describes her estranged husband, Prince Charles, as 'the great white hope' and the royal family as 'the leper colony'? What to make of a princess who vows that she wants to take on the world, and then withdraws from it; a wife exultant in escaping the iron clutches of a desperately unhappy union, then vacillating about the final parting of the ways? What to make of a disillusioned royal, who tells friends, 'I've got to get out of this hellhole', and yet seems reluctant to hand back her tiara?

3

The Princess of Wales's honest confusion and soul-searching as she has tried to come to terms with her new status as a fallen idol has been watched by a worldwide audience, eager to reassess a woman who was, until her separation, seen as an exquisite enigma, an adored holy Madonna, whose elusive personality was a blank canvas on which we were invited to paint our fantasies and dreams. Since those innocent days of a doe-eyed Diana collecting posies from children, which now seem as distant as Mrs Thatcher in her pomp, this regal goddess has demonstrated, all too publicly, that, when the glossy veneer is stripped away, there is a flawed human being beneath, prone to doubt and indecision, and vulnerable to criticism. Living legends bleed too. 'I'm not a slab of meat,' complained Marilyn Monroe shortly before her tragic death, a sentiment echoed by the princess, whose earnest desire is to establish herself as a personality in her own right.

Since the Waleses' separation in December 1992, the princess and her husband have been judged on a daily basis by a jury of the press and public, whose fickle moods and arbitrary censure tell us much about society, and, in particular, its inability to deal with a woman who will not conform to a stereotype. The royal separation released, as one commentator noted, 'a backlash of misogynous indignation that was truly shocking'. Diana has been by turns alarmed, indignant and frustrated as she has seen what she believes to be the truth of her case scorned or ignored by the media and public as she has rather

4

belatedly realized the limitations of her position. Indeed the debate surrounding the OJ Simpson case in America echoes the televised confession of adultery by the Prince of Wales. Both incidents raise the question of how society comes to terms with its 'heroes' when they transgress. The enthusiastic support for the former pro-football star who became, for a time, a fugitive from justice mirrors the popular acclamation and praise for the 'courage and honesty' the prince displayed in admitting that he had cheated on his wife for most of his marriage. Diana knows full well that if she had made a similar confession she would have been branded an 'unfit mother' and subjected to bilious attack by an assortment of self-righteous Members of Parliament, churchmen and columnists.

This is no exaggeration. When the infamous 'toe-sucking' pictures of the already separated Duchess of York were released, Fergie found herself subject to a quasi-ritual public humiliation. If Diana was caught in a careless caress or innocent embrace with a man who is not her husband, she knows that the whispering campaign would begin. It is her greatest concern that her children will be taken away from her by the most influential and feared family in Britain. While Charles can discuss his friendship with Camilla Parker Bowles, the princess knows that one royal convention she cannot break is the unwritten rule that she must not take another man. So, for example, she never has dinner parties at Kensington Palace for fear they may be misconstrued, any unattached men present becoming fair game for an ever-watchful media.

It is an unhealthy situation, compounded by her emotional nature. The princess is a tactile, affectionate woman who longs for the warmth and companionship that a loving relationship brings but has been denied her for so long. Yet her anxiety instinctively inhibits her forming new emotional attachments as long as the current status quo exists. Locked into a cool and distant marriage for most of her adult life, the princess has channelled her affections elsewhere. Giving extravagant presents is one way of showing that affection and she surrounds herself with material possessions to cushion her isolation. She is overly protective of her sons in the way many single-parent mothers are, overly familiar with her staff because she is lonely, and unnervingly open with total strangers she comes across in her charity work. As a friend observes: 'She is always doing everything for everybody else, she needs to start doing things for herself. She wants the praise and adulation for being a martyr because of her great insecurity.' This characteristic was noted by columnist, Lynda Lee-Potter, when the princess returned from her tour of Zimbabwe in July 1993:

She has embarked on this life of service with fanatical fervour. It has become a substitute for the loving marriage she craved . . . Undeniably there is room in her life for the work which obsesses her. But unless she begins to have time for herself, and the courage to become vulnerable again, she will never grow into a complete and personally fulfilled human being.

When she read the article Diana ruefully acknowledged the sentiments expressed: 'Well, that hit the nail on the head didn't it?'

A manifestation of this dysfunctional life is her frenetic round of exercise and therapies, this ersatz attention a hollow substitute for genuine love and affection. She seeks solace in consultations with her astrological counsellor whose musings on the fate of Prince Charles and her own fate bolster her feelings of renewal and optimism in the lonely world she inhabits. Starved of love, she pays for sensual pleasures in what she calls her 'Pamper Diana' days, where a variety of therapists treat her to the delights of deep-tissue massage, aromatherapy, acupuncture, cranial massage and osteopathy. In her lonely life, her most faithful friend is the telephone. She spends many hours a day chatting to friends, pouring out her sorrows and ruminating about her estranged husband and the rest of the royal family. This need for company, even at a distance, has savagely rebounded on her. In August 1994, she was accused of making nuisance phone calls to her friend, art dealer Oliver Hoare. While she vigorously denied the charge, friends recognized obsessive telephoning as part of a continuing pattern of need.

Her global celebrity merely sharpens this sense of emotional isolation, every day experiencing the loneliness that only a living phenomenon can truly understand. 'She feels that she is in a prison, not just a goldfish bowl but, within her own experience, a prison with no way out and no shoulder to cry on. It is a terrible space to be in,' says an adviser. In her palace fastness Diana knows that every time she leaves the safety of her front door she makes herself a hostage to fortune. Her vulnerability makes her constantly anxious about her place and position. She cancelled a trip to the cinema to watch *What's Love Got to Do with It?* about singer Tina Turner's life which involved her violent relationship with her husband in case it was misconstrued. 'Not a clever idea,' Diana argued. Instead she dines alone or with her butler or watches television—and the circle of isolation is complete. 'I feel very lonely at the moment, very strange. I feel that I have shed something major in my life,' she said to a friend shortly after her withdrawal from public life. It is a solitude she shares with that other goddess who has fallen on hard times, the pop star, Madonna. Too famous to go out she will sit in a hotel room after a concert while everyone else enjoys the party. 'You feel the most unbelievable loneliness. Yes, everyone adores you in a kind of mass-energy way, but then you're absolutely separated from humanity. It's the most bizarre irony.' For Diana perhaps the most poignant of many such moments was on Christmas Day 1993. She was all smiles as she greeted the crowd outside Sandringham Church and then, as agreed, left Princes William and Harry with their father and the rest of the royal family at the Queen's Norfolk retreat.

The princess returned to an empty Kensington Palace where her chef, Mervyn Wycherley, had left her Christmas lunch. She ate alone before going for a solitary swim at Buckingham Palace. Then, the following day, she boarded a plane and flew to Washington to spend a week with her friend Lucia Flecha de Lima, the wife of the Brazilian ambassador. Then the mask slipped. As she recalls: 'I cried all the way out and all the way back, I felt so sorry for myself.' It was a similar routine the following year but with a happier outcome—she enjoyed a week's skiing in Colorado without the attendant blizzard of paparazzi photographers.

Thwarted by her position from finding a new love, the princess dwells on the past and what she has lost. She feels profound anger at the position she finds herself in, endlessly exasperated by the 'unfairness'—a word she uses often—of her lot. Her sense of outrage is directed against an institution whose standards and values she believed in and which betrayed her; bitterness towards a husband who rejected her for another and indignation towards those, especially in the media, who refuse to acknowledge what she sees as the injustice of her situation. She looks back on her carefree bachelor time at Coleherne Court as 'the happiest days of my life'. As she recalls: 'Before I married into the royal family I didn't know about jealousy or depressions or unhappiness. I had such a wonderful existence as a kindergarten teacher, you never thought of anything like that.'

The princess grieves a failed marriage and a lost innocence, while continuing her stumbling, sometimes painful search for a new life. 'She was a sweet and innocent bloom cruelly deceived,' argues a friend. 'They expected her to be a living sacrifice for the monarchy while Charles was busy cheating behind her back. She has wasted her adult life living a lie.' It was no coincidence that when Diana was sent a copy of the book, *The Charm Syndrome*, which details how men of high social status systematically isolate and then manipulate their women, the princess read it from cover to cover in a day. During the marriage she expressed her frustrations in shouting matches with Prince Charles and, when they wearied of the battle, she would go to her bedroom and beat her bed with a tennis racquet. Or she would get into her car and go for a high-speed burn-up until she had cooled down. Now photographers face the lash of her tongue while her exploration of numerous New-Age therapies allows her to channel her rage. Her regular colonic irrigations, a water treatment that flushes out toxins from the bowel, are a tonic because, as she says, 'they take all the aggro out of me.' Every Thursday she visits a Beauchamp Place clinic for a colonic and also for 'anger release' sessions where Welsh therapist, Chryssie Fitzgerald, encourages her to shout and scream, venting her fury on a punch-bag. This has developed into a full-scale boxing workout with a black boxer friend of Chryssie Fitzgerald's. The princess exercises regularly with weights to strengthen her upper arms for these strenuous sessions. This need to come to terms with the demons within has led her along shady byways in the world of New-Age therapy. At Kensington Palace she was visited by Harley Street hypnotherapist, Roderick Lane, later identified as a bookbinder at Windsor Castle. He would talk to her about visualizing her anger, throwing it up an imaginary chimney and then burning it.

Her soothsayers forecast that 1994 would be the year to deal with the anger she feels, a shorthand for saying that Diana would now be able to let go of the past and forge ahead in a new direction. At times she uses her sense of anger as a crutch and a barrier against moving on, displaying again her self-imposed martyrdom. During the winter of 1993, for example, the business motivation guru, Anthony Robbins, offered to give her a private seminar in a Washington hotel. He and his wife had previously met the princess at Kensington Palace and there was much mutual admiration. She liked his drive, energy and optimism while the millionaire lecturer sensed that beyond the veil of suffering and sadness which surrounds the princess there lurked a brave and strong woman who had already demonstrated a willingness to take on difficult issues and challenges. The plan came to nought for many reasons, one being her belief that she had to deal with her anger before she could undertake this kind of intensive tuition which had the potential to give her a more positive outlook on life.

A sense of how deep her anger runs is shown by her flirtation with Roman Catholicism. She has a number of Catholic friends including Rosa Monckton, Lucia Flecha de Lima and Mother Teresa of Calcutta, and the princess enjoys the ceremonial side of the service. She believes that in a previous incarnation she was a nun and is aware that one of her Spencer ancestors could be made a saint. However, what really engaged her interest was the notion that, under the Catholic creed, her marriage could be annulled on the grounds that her husband had taken his marriage vows cynically, since Diana believed that Charles was involved with another woman at the time. She could plead that, then aged twenty, she was not mature enough to understand truly the significance of the step she was taking. It was a seductive but ultimately fanciful idea. It was pointed out that if her marriage were annulled her children would be illegitimate. She has now dismissed the notion. 'I've as much chance of becoming Buddhist or becoming a Muslim as converting to Catholicism,' she has told friends.

This need to avenge her rejection is matched by her continued obsession with the relationship that cast a long shadow over her marriage. While she affects an indifference to the fate of Prince Charles and Camilla Parker Bowles, she watches their every move like a hawk and gleans every scrap of gossip about them that she can. Just months after the separation, she discovered where they conducted their meetings. She obtained a large-scale Ordnance Survey map, pinpointed the house and then worked out the routes they used to avoid detection. With one of her soothsayers, she will plot Camilla's astrological chart—

like Diana she is Cancerian—and then she mulls over the runes. She ponders their fate with a brooding and morbid fascination, asking herself and her friends if they will find happiness together, or if he will ever have the courage to give up the throne for the woman Diana believes he loves. At times she has sympathy for their plight. 'He won't give her up and I wish him well,' she told a friend. 'I would like to say that to his face one day.' Camilla is equally transfixed by her rival's behaviour, gloating over media criticism of the princess, angered when she herself is condemned. When my book *Diana, Her True Story* was made in to a film, she secretly watched a video of the movie, hiding it down the back of a sofa in the drawing room. This cat-and-mouse game continually opens old wounds, especially when the princess is confronted by independent evidence of her husband's methodical and long-running betrayal. That mood easily turns to reproach. Days after Jonathan Dimbleby's documentary, *Charles: The Private Man, The Public Role*, was televised in June 1994, where he was praised for his 'courage' in admitting his adultery, Brenda Stronach, the former wife of Charles's valet told a Sunday newspaper how Charles's staff and the police at Highgrove conspired to deceive Diana about her husband's friendship. She revealed that they routinely used to lie to the princess about his whereabouts, even covering up a car accident in which the prince was involved, and disclosed that a favourite ploy of the prince's was to circle programmes in the TV listings magazine, *Radio Times*, so that Diana

13

would get the impression that he had spent a quiet night at home. The constant duplicity was such a strain on the health of Prince Charles's valet, Ken Stronach, that he suffered from intense headaches.

Brenda Stronach, who watched these activities, commented: 'It was a deceitful and cruel conspiracy. I used to feel sorry for the poor girl. It used to break my heart to see the state she got herself into.' When the princess read the story it brought painful and bitter memories flooding back. Simmering with rage, she penned Prince Charles a curt note: 'May I dismiss these comments as lies? Highgrove was my home too.' She remembered that, when she first questioned the staff about her husband's adultery, they had said her suspicions were unfounded. When her friends had spoken about Charles's friendship, they were accused of exaggerating. Finally, Diana was dismissed as 'mentally unstable' for harbouring such thoughts—a ploy successfully used in Communist Russia when dealing with awkward intellectuals.

It was but another sniping salvo in a relationship that has deteriorated into mutual suspicion. Their regrets about the breakdown of their marriage are expressed to their friends—or television cameras— but not to each other. They are happy, too, to point out each other's weaknesses to others. At the wedding of Princess Margaret's daughter, Lady Sarah Armstrong-Jones, the princess went to the church service, which was watched by enthusiastic crowds and the media, and missed the reception which was held in private at Clarence House, the Queen Mother's London home. In a sardonic aside to the Queen during the church service, Prince Charles remarked that it was interesting that Diana had chosen to attend the public rather than the private aspect of the ceremony even though she had retired from public life. Nor did her appearance by the church door, conveniently near the official camera position, pass unnoticed by her estranged husband. Diana can be just as bitchy. When she and the boys visited a friend's house they were looking at a number of landscapes painted by an amateur. 'They are not as good as daddy's,' they said loyally. The princess replied: 'Ah, but he's had lots of help.'

It rankles that, while she is struggling to come to terms with her present life, her husband seems to be unconcerned about her fate. 'So you lived to tell the tale,' was an oft-quoted remark he made to a woman who confessed that she had also met the Princess of Wales. This public put-down reflects his private insouciance. When one of the guests at a dinner party lamented that he would like to win back his estranged wife, Charles interjected: 'Well, I don't.' These days she makes so little impression on his life that when she rang to thank him for her birthday present—she is now thirty-three—he couldn't remember what it was. In fact it was a floral straw hat and the princess got the distinct impression it had been purchased by a member of his staff.

Diana is a woman scorned but also a woman forlorn. As a young girl from a broken home she vowed that she would marry only for love, and would never divorce. Even though they are separated, she will never forget the early days when her married life held such promise and hope. She is still his wife and will always be the mother of his children. Her mothering instincts, which initially attracted Charles to her, are powerful. Instead of getting on with her own life, she endlessly frets and worries about his plans, his health and his public image, wondering if he will be king. These sentiments are kindled, not just by her ambition and their rivalry, but the residual affection she still feels for the Prince of Wales. 'He looks very grey,' she will say, and becomes vexed about his heavy workload in the way she did during their courtship. 'When will he learn?' she clucked affectionately when told that he had injured himself once again during a polo match. There are a number of her circle who feel that she still loves him, believing that if he ate enough humble pie, praised her for her achievements and apologized for his adultery, she would take him back. A friend who asked precisely that question recalled her reply: 'I would be absolutely shaken and would forgive him.' It is a chimera. Distance and the passage of time lend a glow to the past, the good times recalled more vividly, and less accurately.

Her instinctive impulse to forgive, the traditional handmaiden of anger, hints at the tragedy of their failed relationship. As she mourns her unfulfilled life, tears of grief catch her by surprise. The princess found herself crying one evening as she watched the romantic film, *Indecent Proposal*, about a rich man, played by Robert Redford, who offers the happily married Demi Moore $1 million to sleep with him. While she accepted the offer, in the end true love prevailed and she was reconciled with her caring and protective husband, played by *Cheers* actor, Woody Harrelson. His line, 'I wouldn't share my wife with anyone', touched a chord in Diana's heart and she found herself reaching for the tissues.

Innocent remarks cut deep, reopening the wounds in her heart. When she heard the boys say: 'Daddy really does love you, mummy,' on their return from Highgrove, she found herself gulping back the tears. Her sons are a source of constant consolation and, particularly Prince William, a focus for her ambitions. However, when they are with her she sees what she has lost, and when they are away she realizes how little she can influence the way they now live their lives. The boys, particularly William, sense that. While she protects them—their welfare is the first consideration in all legal negotiations—they are increasingly protective towards her, for example refusing to cooperate with photographers if they feel they have treated 'mummy' badly. 'Why doesn't daddy protect her?' William once asked.

Naturally a shy, sensitive boy, William has suffered the deepest hurt in the emotional upheaval of the last few years. For a time his schoolwork suffered and the princess saw Gerald Barber, the headmaster of Ludgrove School, to discuss a patch of poor exam results. At first sight the princes are like any other boisterous schoolboys. They spend their time go-carting, cycling and playing computer games. 'They're just like normal children and really nice to get on with,' says fellow go-carter, Gareth Howell. 'They like exactly the same things as other boys their age.' Except that they never can be like other boys. At school they are the only boys with detectives, the only pupils allowed to use the headmaster's study to phone their mother each Sunday, the only ones who have locks on their tuck boxes, telling their schoolfriends to hide letters 'from the enemy'. William's sometimes grave expression, his unnatural caution and emotional maturity befit his future role. When the princess was offered a position with the RSPCA, an animal protection charity, her elder son, who loves shooting, advised her to turn it down. 'Every time I kill anything they will blame you,' he observed astutely. She accepted his counsel, telling friends proudly: 'Sometimes he comes out with the expressions of a thirty-year-old but then he wants the reassurance all children need.'

While Prince Charles wants the boys to follow in his footsteps and spend time in the Armed Forces, the princess is keen to show her children wider horizons than, for instance, the grouse moors of Balmoral. She is carefully grooming the boys for their destiny, 'breaking them in gently' to public life by encouraging them to make speeches at staff parties and secret visits to her charities. Her ambition extends far beyond the boundaries of teaching them good manners and sensitivity to the feelings of others. In her cups, or at least over a glass of designer water, she hints at a dream that would place the House of Spencer in competition with the House of Windsor. As she tells friends: 'If I was able to write my own script, I would hope that my husband would go off with his lady and leave me and the children to carry the Wales name until William ascends the throne. I'll be behind them all the way.' Her dream, underscored by endless discussions with her soothsayers and counsellors about the possibility of Charles giving up his position, will remain just that—wishful-thinking. Prince Charles and his family are determined that, while Diana may one day be the king's mother, she will never be kingmaker.

However wild her fantasies, the princess has to face the day-to-day reality of her disenfranchised royal status. Not only has she been edged to the margins of royal life, but also she has watched helplessly as the royal family have smoothly undermined her most fulfilling role in life, that of a loving mother. When she discovered that Prince Charles had hired a 'surrogate mother' under the guise of assistant private secretary she could hardly contain her anger. 'Absolutely outrageous,' said a friend, arguing that if she employed a stand-in father for the boys there would be uproar. The arrival of Alexandra 'Tiggy' Legge-Bourke, a girl of a similar age and social status to Diana, and whose mother is lady-in-waiting to Princess Anne, was part of an overall strategy to create an alternative family for the young princes when they are with their father. The noisy, effervescent, former nursery school teacher organizes outings, takes them shopping and keeps them entertained. She liaises with Charles's friends, millionaire racehorse owner Hugh van Cutsem and his wife Emilie, who have also taken on the mantle of substitute parents when Charles is not around; William and Harry regularly stay on their Norfolk estate. These developments were watched in simmering silence by Diana. She winced when she saw newspaper photographs of Harry sitting on Tiggy's knee in the back of a car, shuddered at the idea of her calling the boys 'my babies' and grimaced when she learned that she had taken them to buy Prince Charles a birthday present during a stay at Balmoral. At first she raised the question of Tiggy's relationship with her husband, sending him a handwritten note expressing her concern. Finally she snapped. One weekend Charles was unable to join the boys at Highgrove and left Tiggy in charge. The princess phoned her and told her in no uncertain terms: 'I am the boys' mother, thank you very much.'

Her protests came to nought. A lonely New Year's Day in Washington when she stayed with her friend, Lucia Flecha de Lima, brought home to the princess just how distanced she had become, not just from the royal family but her own children. She phoned Sandringham, where the boys were staying, to wish them a happy New Year. The switchboard operator didn't know where they were and so Diana asked to speak to the Queen. Somewhat perplexed by Diana's ignorance about her sons' whereabouts, the Queen told her that they were with the van Cutsems at

Anmer Hall, which is close to the Queen's winter residence. An embarrassed Diana replied that she had forgotten momentarily where they were.

Her ambitions for her sons lie in confusion, her own royal life in limbo. For the last two years, she has been locked in a custody battle, not just for her children, but for the hearts and minds of the British public. She has carried that fight to the Palace, the prince and the media as she has struggled for emancipation. She has tried to overcome the demons in her marriage, and within herself. The Princess of Wales is learning to be a woman in her own right: a player rather than a puppet, and, further, an individual rather than an icon.

2

'Be True to Yourself'

THE MOST FAMOUS BLUE EYES IN THE WORLD opened wide with disbelief and wry amusement as the man she called 'my tiger' assessed her financial future. 'Do you know how much your husband is worth?' asked Paul Butner, the obscure London lawyer hired by the Princess of Wales to handle her separation from Prince Charles. 'Well, you are entitled to half of it.'

It was an awe-inspiring prospect even for a girl brought up amid the aristocratic splendour of Althorp House in Northamptonshire. The fifty-six-year-old lawyer chosen from a short-list of five drawn up by Diana's friends was adamant about her strong negotiating position, and determined that his client, who went under the alias of Mrs Walsh, should not be steamrollered by the Palace machine. Little wonder that she described him to her friends as 'a real fighter'.

In Butner's view, the princess was perfectly entitled to ask for half the value of Highgrove, the Gloucestershire home Prince Charles had bought from the Macmillan family fifteen years previously, which is estimated to be worth £3 million, half the portfolio of stocks, shares and equities worth over £20 million, as well as a sizeable slice of the £4 million annual income from the Duchy of Cornwall, the estates vested in every Prince of Wales since 1337. As for the 130,000 rolling acres of Duchy-owned farmland and buildings spread across twenty-three counties—including the famous Oval cricket ground in Kennington, south London—well, that could be a useful negotiating counter if the princess wanted to be difficult. During clandestine meetings in offbeat Thai and Chinese restaurants in the autumn of 1993, the princess and her lawyer were discussing multimillion settlement figures—£15 million would be a reasonable sum.

But Diana learned quickly that there is no such thing as a free lunch, especially in dealings with the royal family. While 'the pennies' as Diana called the financial arrangements were important, she had more immediate concerns on her mind during the turbulent final months of 1992: namely, her children, her home and her own personal survival. She had faced a sustained and draining emotional battering from both inside and outside the royal family since the publication that summer of my book, *Diana, Her True Story*, which described her loveless union to Prince Charles, his relationship with another woman, Camilla Parker Bowles, and Diana's isolation within the royal family. Accusations of collusion had brought the wrath of the family upon her.

In the months since June 1992 she had wrestled with so many doubts and fears. She had long exercised extreme caution in all aspects of her life, but in this drastically changed climate, with a whispering campaign against her echoing along the corridors of Buckingham Palace and then bellowed in banner newspaper headlines, she was at a loss about whom to trust. Aristocrats she had called friends repaid her trust with hostile leaks to the media, royal courtiers who once greeted her with a smile now averted their eyes, and as for the royal family she now learned first-hand the truth of the old saying: blood is thicker than water. She was swamped with advice from well-meaning friends and outright hostility from her husband, his family and their friends. 'She has betrayed her husband, her family and her class,' sniffed a senior member of one of Britain's most patrician families.

The cruel change in attitudes towards the Princess of Wales stemmed from her decision finally to confront the tortured reality of her eleven-year marriage to the heir to the throne, rather than continue playing a simpering, smiling role in a ridiculous charade. The elaborate myth of togetherness was slowly suffocating her inner spirit, her self-respect and her very existence. By ripping asunder the curtain of hypocrisy surrounding her marriage, Diana revealed the double standards within the institution of monarchy. The refrain, which was repeated in the drawing rooms of the upper classes and was trumpeted across the pages of the chintzier broadsheet newspapers, ran on the following lines: 'She knew what she was getting in to', 'That's the way the aristocracy have always lived', 'With all her privileges why is she complaining?' and 'Why didn't she quietly take a lover herself and turn a blind eye to Prince Charles and his mistress?' Diana had let the side down by her refusal to continue with this lie. Naturally this begged the question what kind of 'side' was it that placed a higher premium on deception than on honesty, subterfuge as opposed to openness, despondency rather than happiness.

Within this unsympathetic social climate both the Princess of Wales and the Duchess of York privately tussled with the collapse of their marriages and their disillusion with the royal system. For more than a decade, Diana had submerged her own character as she performed the traditional duties of the Princess of Wales supremely well, investing royalty with a glamour and appeal not seen since the days of Queen Alexandra. Both the princess and the duchess come from a new generation of women who are unwilling to accept the yoke of unhappy marriages and social circumstances for ever. As Zelda West Meads, the one-time voice of the marriage guidance agency,

Relate, and one of Diana's circle observes: 'One of the biggest changes over the years has been that women are not prepared to put up with bad marriages for any longer than they need to. They say to me, "I only have one life and I don't want to be trapped in this relationship for most of it."'

Over many months of anguished heart-searching they concluded, with regret, that the self-sacrifice required to sustain an empty and unhappy union for the sake of the monarchy, an institution they had come to see with a mixture of cynicism and fear, was no longer worth it. 'We're both chained to our stupid duties and ruining our lives together,' the duchess told her husband during one exasperated phone conversation. 'It was like being trapped in a Grimm brothers' nightmare,' the duchess observed.

The volatility of their marriages was such that, when I was researching *Diana, Her True Story* during 1991, it was decided to bring forward publication from September to June 1992 as royal separations seemed imminent. It was clear that both the Duchess of York and Princess of Wales frequently discussed leaving the royal family, either separately or together. The Queen, although alert to the difficulties they faced, was less than sympathetic. 'You egg each other on,' she told Diana during one meeting at Sandringham.

There were endless conversations between the princess and duchess as they mulled over their options. The advice from the assorted ranks of astrologers, mystics, clairvoyants and tarot-card readers was a faulty thread in the weft and weave of their unhappy lives, strongly disapproved of by the Queen. One day Fergie might telephone Diana to warn her that her astrologer forecast an accident involving a royal car. Predictions by their mediums forecast variously that Prince Andrew would become king or indicated that the Queen Mother's life was in danger. Indeed, much store was set by the princess and the duchess on the health of the Queen Mother. They saw her as the linchpin of the entire edifice of monarchy, believing that her demise would seriously jeopardize Prince Charles's chances of ever becoming king. His resolve to rule would evaporate as the dynasty collapsed. These predictions added an aura of unreality to the musings of two women already living in the bizarre looking-glass world of royal life. It was hardly surprising that on the day the Duchess of York decided to leave the royal family, she consulted the Greek mystic, Madame Vasso, for advice, rather than a royal courtier.

The Yorks' separation in March 1992 made Diana's position all the more precarious, focusing attention on the emptiness of her own marriage and the Waleses' obvious public discomfiture. There was also growing speculation about the contents of my book. Fergie's departure and her subsequent isolation by the royal family—'the knives are out for the Duchess of York at Buckingham Palace' one senior courtier told the BBC—forced Diana to think very seriously about her own future. 'At least I've been true to myself,' the duchess said after she had had an uncomfortable audience with the Queen at Sandringham. It was a sentiment which Diana was to wrestle with throughout the summer of 1992.

For months the Princess of Wales, described as 'the mistress of the coded message', had waged a subtle operation to give the public some sense of her disaffection. An unhappy visit to India in the spring of 1992 publicly revealed the fissures in her marriage. While Diana had happily posed alone by the Taj Mahal, the monument to lost love, Charles addressed a business meeting. The distance between the couple was underlined when the princess deliberately turned away as the prince tried to kiss her following a polo match in Jaipur. Not for the first—or last—time Diana used her body language to devastating effect. While this silent public sniping may have wounded the prince it did not constitute a full-scale assault.

As the weeks passed, Fergie's words constantly returned to haunt the princess. How, though, could she be true to herself if she didn't really know who the real Diana was? Throughout her formative twenties, she had been content to be moulded and manipulated by her husband, royal courtiers and the media. She looked to them for approval and applause. If it failed to materialize, it merely fed her profound sense of failure and rejection, feelings seated in an unhappy childhood dominated by her parents' acrimonious divorce. For much of her life Diana had seen herself as the helpless victim of circumstances, unable or unwilling to alter the conditions which shackled her. These character defects which stopped Diana from taking control of her own life were exacerbated by the genteel institutional life inside Kensington Palace. It wasn't simply the spy cameras, the eavesdropping staff and watchful police, which tethered the 'prisoner of Wales', but the 'puppet culture', where Diana was consistently disenfranchised from decisions affecting her life; she may well have given the appearance of being in control, but she was in the iron grip of her diary and her courtiers. Daily decisions were made affecting her every move. If she overstepped the boundaries she would face a hostile memo or interview from the Queen's private secretary, Sir Robert Fellowes.

At home and abroad, Diana had to obey these 'rules' of royal behaviour. For example, an innocent drink with actress Liza Minnelli at a party following a royal film premiere was deemed 'inappropriate' behaviour and her frequent lunches at the fashionable Italian restaurant, San Lorenzo, thought to be 'excessive'. If she wanted to fly outside Britain, Diana first had to obtain permission from the Queen. Fergie was to spend a dismal wet few days with her children, Princesses Eugenie and Beatrice, in an empty hotel in Torquay during February 1993 because the Palace refused to allow her to fly to the West Indies to stay in a chalet she had already booked and paid for. They argued that, as the Princess of Wales had been pictured in a bikini in the Caribbean a few weeks before, they did not want to take the risk of the duchess making a similar exhibition of herself.

Prone to procrastination and unused to exercising

free will, Diana was watched by her circle of friends with much nervousness that summer. On the one hand they saw her profound unhappiness, but knew that, at least for the moment, she was paralysed. She was stifled by her upbringing, which had taught her deference, and her nature, which veered on the side of caution. 'She is not a congruent person,' noted a friend, meaning that the discordant core of her personality prevented her heart, instincts and head functioning in harmony. Little by little, her growing sense of self-belief and her urgent impulse to burst free of her claustrophobic life urged her on to action; she also gained inspiration from watching the Duchess of York deal with her problems. She was beginning to realize that once she had come to terms with her failed relationship, then she could fully develop as an individual.

Yet neither the prince nor the princess could have foreseen the dragon of public debate they were about to unleash when they sat down in their drawing room at Kensington Palace on 8 June 1992 to rake over the rubble of their relationship. From that moment, Diana boarded an emotional rollercoaster, a ride which only came to a temporary halt when the separation was announced in December.

Even at this relatively short remove, it is difficult to recall the intensity of media interest, public absorption and high anxiety among Diana's friends and supporters during those ten days in June 1992, which shattered the fairytale and rocked the British monarchy. The rapid tempo of events behind the closed doors of Kensington Palace was matched by gathering hysteria in the British Establishment and the media. The serialization in the *Sunday Times* of my book, *Diana, Her True Story*, was headlined: 'Diana driven to five suicide bids by "uncaring" Charles'. It went on to make three sensational assertions: that the Princess of Wales had suffered from the eating disorder, bulimia nervosa; that she had made several half-hearted attempts to take her own life; and that from the moment he took his marriage vows Prince Charles had enjoyed a secret relationship with another woman, Camilla Parker Bowles.

The first couple of weeks following serialization were hectic, and clearly revealed the strengths and weaknesses of the royal protagonists in this protracted drama. As the public absorbed the twists and turns in the marriage crisis, events moved inexorably to a climax within palace walls. On the same day as the serialization began, the Queen was the guest of honour at Windsor Great Park to watch Prince Charles play polo. Her gesture in inviting Camilla Parker Bowles and her husband Andrew to join her in the Royal Enclosure on the day that the nation was digesting the implications of the Waleses' unhappy marriage, was seen by Diana's circle as a graphic remonstration against the princess.

At the same time the Establishment and their media acolytes were in full cry. Lord McGregor, the chairman of the Press Complaints Commission, issued a statement condemning the hysteria surrounding the book as: 'An odious exhibition of journalists dabbling their fingers in the stuff of other people's souls.' This criticism was never made of the book itself and Lord McGregor has since told me that the issue was the 'most difficult' of his tenure. The Archbishop of Canterbury worried about the effects of the publicity on Princes William and Harry; Lord Fawsley, a former leader of the House of Commons, condemned the publication and a potpourri of Members of Parliament sweetly suggested that I be sent to the Tower of London; it was a torrid time for Diana's supporters.

Meanwhile at Kensington Palace on Monday 8 June, the royal couple met in sombre mood to discuss their future. Unknown to Diana, Prince Charles had already made the first decisive move. The previous day he had seen the Queen at Windsor Castle and frankly discussed the consequences of a divorce. She had long been aware of the breakdown of her son's relationship with his wife, but nevertheless was concerned about the impact on her grandchildren, her son's public image and the monarchy. After some heart-searching, they concluded that the legal wheels could be set in motion and the name of Lord Goodman, the distinguished lawyer, was mentioned as a possible constitutional adviser. Before he left, the Queen asked Charles if he and the princess could actually bear to sit down together and discuss the issue rationally. As a close friend noted: 'The Queen knew only too well that the simple act of getting the Waleses to talk at all was a miracle.'

For once that miracle was achieved and the royal

couple coolly and calmly discussed the repercussions of a separation. A diary kept by a friend of the Princess of Wales during the tense days gives an insight into Diana's state of mind, and the misgivings she began to feel about achieving a separation once she saw the depth of animosity of the royal family and its supporters. The following entry gives a flavour of the release of tension between them once the fateful decision to part had been made.

Diana and Charles agreed that they were incompatible and decided on a parting of the ways. She could see a glimmer of light. Relief that reality of the situation seemed to be faced. It was a sit-down talk triggered by the events of the summer. He was being reasonable, grown-up and himself. He didn't have the others there. No tears. First time Diana slept through night without sleeping pills. Gained enormous strength. Diana phones to say that he agrees [to a separation]. She is elated and can sleep now.

Other friends were equally impressed by Diana's new-found sense of resolve. One observed: 'She has strength and courage and I've never seen her so determined.'

The following day, Tuesday 9 June, Prince Charles flew to Denmark leaving Diana to attend Prince Harry's sports day on her own. While the tension at Kensington Palace was almost palpable, there was a sense of relief among her circle of friends, knowing she had finally embarked on a difficult journey which at least brought her the hope of a happy ending. 'We had seen her miserable for so long. Now there was light at the end of the tunnel,' recalled one confidante. However, there was anxiety that Diana would not have the stamina to stand up to the pressure both inside and outside the royal family. Prone to retreat in the face of attack, Diana's circle realized that it was imperative that she have cool legal counsel to call on in the difficult days ahead.

As her friend recorded in her diary:

Very stressful at Kensington Palace. Diana didn't know what was going on with the family. Chat going on behind closed doors. Still thought that Charles was going forward with discussions with parents. Fellowes rang and told her that she was making his life unbearable. Diana said that she had talked to a couple of close friends about recommending lawyers. The first suggestion was Charles Doughty of the London firm Withers but when she discovered that was Fergie's solicitor she said no. Short list of five drawn up.

The tart conversation with her brother-in-law, Sir Robert Fellowes, concerned her suspected collusion with my book. This turned into downright accusation the following evening when she visited the Fulham home of one of her oldest friends, Carolyn Bartholomew. When she left after a thirty-minute visit, several photographers lay in wait and snapped the scene of the princess kissing her best friend on the doorstep. It was instantly interpreted as confirmation of her involvement. A more innocent explanation that an inquisitive neighbour had tipped off various newspapers was treated with silent disbelief by courtiers. A friend noted Diana's meeting with her sister, Jane Fellowes, in her diary:

Meeting with Fellowes. He reiterated stuff about making his life miserable. She spoke to Jane. Jane came to see her and said: 'I never realized it's been so miserable for you.' She seemed to be more sympathetic.

As the nation awoke to photographs of Carolyn and Diana kissing their farewells, the princess faced a flight to Merseyside to open a hospice. During that highly charged visit she burst into tears when a pensioner in the crowd stroked her face in a spontaneous gesture of affection. Her emotional outburst was expected, as her friend recorded:

Changed mood from press after visit to Carolyn. She really couldn't take much more. Message from Major [Prime Minister] saying that he couldn't help her leave if she tried to manipulate the press. Lots of tears. Feeling exhausted. In the morning she says she was told by R_____ [a friend] that if she wanted to cry in public she should do so. He argued that the world should see the private torment for themselves. Diana said afterwards that when her face was stroked 'that triggered something inside me. I simply couldn't stop myself crying.'

The following day, on the eve of the Trooping the Colour ceremony, where the royal family traditionally gather en masse, Diana was understandably nervous and apprehensive. As her friend noted: 'Diana tired and tearful, exhausted and dreaded meeting the entire family.' Conscious of the symbolism of this time-honoured family gathering on the Buckingham Palace balcony, the princess planned her weekend strategy with some care. As ever she was at her most expressive when the silent eloquence of her body language spoke for her. Her friend recorded:

It was her deliberate intention to step apart from Prince Charles, to leave him in the background. But not the Queen. She stayed close to her to show her ultimate allegiance to the Crown. Afterwards she felt that it had gone well. She didn't want anybody to get the impression that they were back together again. Atmosphere: cold and flat. Very unfriendly and uncomfortable. On Sunday Diana feeling tired. Strong climate against her inside the family and now she knew how stiff things could be.

It was just as difficult for the other members of the royal family. According to one participant, it was 'extremely uncomfortable'. Diana did find one royal supporter, though, in her next-door neighbour, Princess Michael of Kent, who had long been the butt of family jokes because of her statuesque bearing, her Catholicism and unusual pedigree: 'You are much too good for this family,' she told her. While the weekend with the royal family was bleak, she approached with more trepidation the week-long stay at Windsor Castle during the Ascot race meeting, where she and Prince Charles had arranged to discuss their marriage situation with the Queen and the Duke of Edinburgh. Before that, she had to attend the Garter ceremony where, as her friend noted in her diary, Diana sensed that Prince Charles's resolution was beginning to waver.

At the Garter ceremony Charles kept saying to her: 'It's very difficult, it's very difficult.' Now she is beginning to question his ability to carry through what they both want under his own steam. The meeting with the in-laws was worse than she expected. Left her shaken rigid. They accused her of having done the book. More than that they impressed on her the fact that they had proof of her involvement with book and the newspapers. Diana was asked: 'Did she know a man called Andrew Knight?' [The then chief executive of News International, publishers of the Sunday Times.] Diana was told: 'We have a recording of a commentary by a man called Andrew Knight.' Diana denied that that was the case. They said that they had a tape of her discussing serialization with a newspaper and whether it should go to the *Daily Mail* or the *Sunday Times*. Heavily criticized for collusion and bringing family into disrepute. Had she helped: 'No.' A lot of tears. Prince Philip angry, raging and unpleasant. During meeting she turned to Prince Charles and said: 'Tell them Charles what you want to say.' He just stood there absolutely stum. Diana said: 'We discussed all this on Monday.' Again silence. Diana said afterwards: 'It was as though this conversation never happened.' She emphasized her total astonishment that he couldn't speak for himself when his parents were present. His physical proximity leaves her cold.

Bemused, battered and bewildered, Diana sought out Sir Robert Fellowes, seeking clarification on the vexed issue of an alleged tape recording. Her mind reeled with the possibilities. Could the Queen, or her advisers, really have authorized the tapping of her daughter-in-law's phone conversations? Too outrageous even to be contemplated. Diana knew that these alleged conversations had never taken place so assumed it was simply an elaborate bluff to extract a confession from her. When she spoke to the Queen's private secretary he told her that there was indeed a tape but advised her to do nothing. The following day he informed her to forget all about the tape as it could not, or would not, be used against her. As far as he was concerned the issue was closed.

This is a perplexing incident. When I was told about it literally within hours of the Windsor Castle meeting by several unimpeachable sources, both my publisher and I found it so far-fetched as to be unbelievable. It seemed all the more absurd since my publisher, Michael O'Mara, had personally negotiated the serialization with the *Sunday Times* in conditions of absolute secrecy. Yet over the next six months three tapes were released of intimate telephone conversations, allegedly between Diana and a male admirer, Prince Charles and Camilla Parker Bowles, and the Duke and Duchess of York. It would be easy, as many have done, to point a finger at the police or the security forces. However, the most likely explanation is that the tape was mentioned as a tactic, a ruse based on hearsay and Palace gossip, which in truth had little substance in fact. Senior courtiers at Buckingham Palace had been contacted by a News International executive informing them that there was a tape in the *Sunday Times's* safe of the princess being interviewed by myself. While there was no such tape in existence, there was a recording in the safe of the *Sun* newspaper of Diana speaking to a male admirer, widely believed to be James Gilbey. It seems that even the Queen is not immune to receiving garbled information gleaned by the ancient but discredited system of Chinese whispers. None the less, this mystifying affair merely served to confirm Diana's suspicions that she was under siege and made her all the more determined to take every precaution against being spied upon. She had already had her rooms at Kensington Palace swept for listening devices and from time to time used a scrambler telephone when making sensitive calls.

The emotional summit with the Queen and the Duke of Edinburgh during Ascot week gives an insight into the characters of the prince and princess. When face-to-face with his parents in difficult circumstances, it seems that Prince Charles is a very different character to his charming, thoughtful public persona. Tongue-tied, overwrought and ineffectual, from an early age his personal feelings and ambitions have been hammered on the stern anvil of duty, family loyalty and his ultimate destiny as the future king. As Diana once observed to a friend: 'He has to sort out his childhood before he can sort out himself.'

It reveals too a side of Diana's nature which was to assume great importance in future negotiations and decisions. Even though she dismissed Prince Charles as a weak man, paralysed by his parents' dominating presence, Diana herself was always happy for him to take the lead in any dealings with the family. While she criticized him for failing to articulate their common desire to separate, she too was deferential both to her husband and her in-laws, her silence speaking volumes about her upbringing. This is not surprising in the least, coming as she did from an homogeneous upper-class culture that groomed girls to play a supportive role, substantial but none the less secondary, relegated more to jam-making than decision-taking. Aristocratic girls were expected to fall in love and then fall in line.

Diana's education may not have been in the Classics, but was classic in approach: private boarding schools, French finishing school and London cookery course. As Peter York wrote in *The Official Sloane Ranger Handbook*:

Finishing schools are like geisha school: you are supposed to emerge adept at mystic social graces which fit you to spend evenings with the highest in the land, a haven of calm and chaste solace after their days wielding power. You then marry one and are able to do the flowers, direct the cook in French and run a large house.

The princess articulated the underlying acceptance of her subordinate position during the television interview in 1985 with Sir Alastair Burnet. 'I feel my role is supporting my husband whenever I can, and always being behind him, encouraging him. And also, most important being a mother and a wife.' Diana's poor academic record merely underscores her innate submissiveness when dealing with matters of policy, forward planning or argument. While her emotional instincts are profound and penetrating, intellectually she, even two years ago, was all too prone to defer to a man, especially a man with paper qualifications or a veneer of learning.

While this stormy drama unfolded behind castle walls, the ceremony of the first day of Ascot, where the royal family parades past the crowd in horse-drawn carriages, continued its unruffled progress.

Diana felt both 'tickled and embarrassed' when she was cheered to an echo while the Queen and the other royals enjoyed only scattered support. As the princess acknowledged the applause, her carriage companion, the Queen Mother, sat in uncomfortable silence. Never an ally of Diana's—the princess describes social occasions at Clarence House as 'grim and stilted'—the Queen Mother was 'stone cold' towards her granddaughter-in-law. There were other signs that the family fractures had spilled over into the changeless Ascot ceremonial. The estranged Duchess of York and her daughters, Princesses Beatrice and Eugenie, stood with the public to watch the carriage procession; the Prince and Princess of Wales twice left the racecourse together in his Aston Martin, only for Diana to decant into her own car waiting a few miles down the road; and the Duke of Edinburgh was seen studiously to ignore the princess in the royal box.

Unlike the Queen Mother, her father-in-law was not content to let a withering silence signal his disapproval. During the course of the next few weeks Diana received four stinging letters from him, by turns bitter, reproachful, conciliatory and condemnatory. The contents of the first were typical, arguing that Diana was far from innocent in the breakdown of her marriage and making the rhetorical point that it was difficult to blame his eldest son for seeking comfort with Camilla Parker Bowles given the debilitating nature of Diana's long-term eating disorder, bulimia nervosa, as well as her volatile personality. In a rather more placatory vein he confessed that he could understand the difficulties she suffered during her childhood as his own early years had been far from happy. These wounding missives left Diana shocked and numb, but, for once, determined to argue her case. Her private secretary, Patrick Jephson, one of her few trusted allies, helped draft formal responses which included her demand that, as a condition of her staying inside the royal family, Prince Charles pack his bags and leave Kensington Palace. Understandably, all this pressure began to weaken her resolve, as her friend noted in her diary:

Strong sense from Diana that she couldn't trust anybody. Leaned on by the Establishment. Patrick Jephson wants it all to cool down. She was getting cold feet, cold about the idea of a lawyer. 'Now is not the right time,' she said. She was backing off. The relentless pressure from Ascot had frightened the life out of her. 'I'll do it my way. That will be right,' she says. But will it?

The letters, the accusations and the rank suspicion were the harbingers of a long fetid summer of intrigue, gossip and character assassination. The image of the House of Windsor as a dutiful, sober and industrious family had for years completely captured the popular imagination. The sudden and dramatic disclosure that their behaviour was no better than any other family's came as an unpleasant surprise. Royal courts and families have always intrigued among themselves and during this period the Windsors showed themselves little different from the Tudors. As one of Diana's circle says: 'She finds them very disloyal. They say one thing one moment and then the next they are at each other's throats. She avoids them and goes out of her way not to get involved.' However, the Princess of Wales, whether she liked it or not, was in the cockpit of this court conspiracy and was a sometimes shocked but always eager recipient of the summer's swirling rumours. Instead of whispers behind the arras, there were endless telephone calls as fact competed with hearsay, truth with lies. Both Diana and Fergie were convinced that there were numerous plots and conspiracies against them. Sometimes their suspicions proved true, on other occasions they believed some wild exaggeration. Even so, a climate of intense suspicion and distrust was created. Frayed tempers and jangled nerves were displayed, as the warring court factions circled each other, watchful, wary and ready to pounce. 'I'm delighted I'm going on holiday,' said one relieved Buckingham Palace official, 'it's like a snake pit in there.'

Earlier in the year, the Duchess of York's decision to leave the royal family had been leaked to a national newspaper. The duchess was convinced that it was a Buckingham Palace plot to discredit her. For a time she even suspected the woman she called 'Little Miss Goody Two Shoes'—the Princess of Wales. Indeed she was so concerned to find the culprit that, using her 'financial adviser', John Bryan, as a negotiator, she offered an exclusive interview to certain journalists if they would reveal the name of the royal 'mole'. She got no takers. Ironically, two years later it was to be the duchess herself who was to come under suspicion when Prince Edward's romance with Sophie Rhys-Jones was revealed in a Sunday tabloid. On that occasion, the Queen and the rest of the royal family rounded on the hapless duchess blaming her for the leak. It caused such a furore that, following a family conference at Windsor Castle one weekend, an irate Prince Edward wrote a terse memo to Prince Andrew virtually ordering him to keep his estranged wife under control and stop her speaking to journalists. This is but a snapshot of the prevailing climate of routine paranoia inside the royal family. Indeed, these days Prince Edward actually employs a senior courtier to detail all the news stories about him and then list all those who could possibly have leaked information. Bitter inquests and acrimonious investigations, occasionally involving police officers from the Royal Protection Squad, are a regular occurrence.

It is little wonder then that the scrambler telephone, the paper shredder and coded conversation are a daily part of Diana's life. Her caution is entirely justified. At Kensington Palace she tears up every scrap of paper knowing that there are those who rummage through her waste bin. There are no limits to the lengths some journalists will go to invade her privacy. When she took a short break at a Spanish hotel in May 1994, local paparazzi searched her room after she had left and sent imprints she had made on hotel notepaper to experts in Paris for analysis.

Those new to this endless game of cat and mouse are easy prey. Shortly after Ascot, Diana's masseur and confidant, Stephen Twigg, publicly warned that unless the conflicts in the princess's life were properly resolved there would be a tragedy—hinting at another suicide attempt. The princess's enemies immediately sprang. Diana was told by courtiers that she had no option but to sack him for breach of confidentiality. Reluctantly she agreed, knowing that she was losing a friendly face and ally who had spoken up for her at a difficult time. He was later reinstated, although he has now left her side to concentrate on his writings on health subjects.

Stephen Twigg's forced dismissal came at a time when Prince Charles's allies were beginning to rally round in earnest. Friends of Prince Charles who had warned him against marrying Diana twelve years before now urged him to kick her out immediately. In this poisonous atmosphere, his Highgrove circle, who had never warmed to the princess, dismissed Diana as a 'megalomaniac', 'clinically mad', 'manipulative and scheming'. During one 'awful' social encounter, one of Prince Charles's aristocratic friends told Diana to go and see a psychiatrist. Charles's circle had known that for the last two years his own desolation had been so complete that he had contemplated a formal separation or even divorce. Indeed, in January 1992 one of them had privately wagered a large sum on their separation by December. At various councils of war, Charles's allies, who described *Diana, Her True Story* as 'the longest divorce petition in history', implored him to authorize the assault on his estranged wife's integrity.

During a barbecue at Highgrove, Charles's country home, his allies sipped their drinks in the June sunshine and discussed a detailed document outlining a strategy for dealing with Diana. It stated that Diana must be confronted about her suspected involvement with *Diana, Her True Story*. This indeed 'happened, as I have already described, when the Queen broached the issue at Windsor Castle. Other suggestions included investigating the republican tendencies of the then *Sunday Times* editor, Andrew Neil, and the publisher Rupert Murdoch. This was a job joyfully undertaken by several rival newspapers. Finally, it was agreed that various friends should be drafted in to articulate Charles's case to the media.

This strategy seemed fine on paper, but in practice retaliation, as they saw it, was not as easy as it seemed. The official conduit of information about the royal family, the Buckingham Palace press office, was totally inappropriate. Furthermore, the prince's Highgrove set, who included the ex-King Constantine of Greece, Conservative Minister Nicholas Soames, Lord and Lady Romsey, the Earl of Shelburne, landowners Hugh and Emilie van Cutsem, former racing driver Jackie Stewart, Lord and Lady Tryon and skiing friends Charles and Patti Palmer-Tomkinson, were socially ill-equipped for engaging in trench warfare through the tabloid press, the primary battleground for the hearts and minds of the British public. The prince too was reluctant to authorize any criticism lest it further tarnish the image of the monarchy. In his view, silence was the best policy. 'The storm will blow itself out,' he argued. His private secretary, Commander Richard Aylard, told journalists: 'He is worried by her volatile and emotional state and therefore he thinks it is totally unfair to attack her.' A member of his circle outlined more difficulties:

His friends know Charles to be kind, dutiful, sympathetic and intellectual and we had to try to get across our fundamental belief that he was married to an unstable, moody, irrational woman who was out of control. We couldn't orchestrate a proper campaign to vindicate him as we didn't have the system or contacts to explain his side of the story.

Initially the response of Charles's camp was patchy, the mood inside Buckingham Palace that of impotent panic. Slowly Charles's sympathizers took it upon themselves to contact the media and give his side of the story. For example, one the most damaging stories in *Diana, Her True Story* concerned Diana's suicide attempt at Sandringham when she was pregnant with Prince William. She threw herself down the stairs during a furious row with Prince Charles after which he left to go riding. His friends pointed out that she was unhurt and was still shouting abuse at him as she picked herself up from the floor. That was why he had left the house to go riding. Charles's friends ridiculed these desperate cries for help as 'amateur melodramatics'. They singled out an occasion on board the Queen's flight when the royal couple were flying from RAF Northolt to Swansea. During an acrimonious discussion Charles insisted that she join him for a holiday in Balmoral. Diana hotly refused, left her seat and locked herself in the aircraft toilet. Shortly afterwards she emerged, blood trickling down her arms, which she smeared over the cabin walls and seats. 'This was not a suicide attempt,' said one of Charles's circle, 'it was just a silly girl trying to gain attention.'

This campaign of derision and disdain enjoyed the willing collusion of numerous newspaper executives. On one occasion a senior editorial figure even faxed a sympathetic story to Charles at Highgrove for his approval. While he initially vetoed the article, that did not prevent its publication some weeks later. Several friends briefed Charles's biographer, Penny Junor, with material for a long article, which painted Diana as an explosive young woman teetering on the brink. (Penny Junor had hoped to be commissioned to write a book, celebrating the twenty-fifth anniversary of the investiture of the Prince of Wales in July 1994. In the event, the prince asked Jonathan Dimbleby, the television journalist, to take on the task of improving his image.) As the daily drip of critical, often downright abusive, articles about Diana developed into a downpour, it was little wonder that her husband's protestations of innocence no longer held water. 'Why don't you ring the papers yourself?' she asked him during one withering exchange. Perhaps the article that stung her most was a waspish profile in the London *Evening Standard*. 'She has become an ego-maniac convinced of her world importance and even her healing powers. Confiding in no one, irrational and isolated, she plots her escape. Prince Charles's friends are bitter and frustrated at the prospect of the royal family held to ransom by a spoilt and increasingly spiteful woman . . . In her confused and childish imagination, her salvation can only come when she has rid herself of her husband. If the monarchy itself has to crash in the process, then so be it.'

It wasn't the unrelentingly unpleasant nature of the portrait which so wounded Diana, but the knowledge that those who still curtsied and bowed to her and called her 'friend' were the architects of the assault. 'I can't believe it, I just can't believe it,' she said in shocked tones when a friend named the guilty parties. For this was the same circle of friends who had condoned Charles's relationship with Camilla Parker Bowles, a union which, in Diana's eyes, was the canker which had eaten away at the heart of her marriage. It was all the more frustrating given the tone of the criticism. If, as Charles's friends contended, she was unstable, her belief that Camilla and Charles had effectively enjoyed a surrogate marriage could be smoothly dismissed as the ravings of a uncontrollably jealous woman. She took comfort in the fact that though they might denigrate her character, the truth would eventually emerge.

The whispered phone calls, the clandestine meetings and the secret gifts between Camilla and Charles were now being explained away in terms of friendship. Yet Diana and her coterie knew of the existence of a cache of love letters and saucy postcards which could not be so easily repudiated. She had come across these billets-doux quite by chance while she and Charles were staying as guests of the Queen on the Balmoral estate. Written on Camilla's headed notepaper, they left the princess in no doubt about the depth of feeling between her husband and the woman he had once wooed, then lost but always loved. Reading them made her feel sick but also gave her the grim satisfaction that her instincts and observations had proved true.

With open warfare declared between the Waleses, Buckingham Palace in turmoil and separation discussions now under way, the grotesque charade of normality continued. A summer cruise, foolishly billed as a 'second honeymoon' for Charles and Diana, was announced. For the princess it was a holiday in hell. Painful memories of previous holidays on board the *Alexander*—one of eleven luxury yachts owned by the Greek billionaire, John Latsis—made it unbearable; her anxious wait for news about her friend, Adrian Ward-Jackson, who was dying of AIDS; overhearing her husband make a ship-to-shore phone call to Camilla; and the simmering anger she felt at a dinner party on board, where Charles led the company in a light-hearted discussion about the value of mistresses. The holiday was organized with military precision—even to the extent of arranging a decoy convoy to leave Kensington Palace to fool the media. Diana, who was joined on board by Princess Alexandra, Sir Angus Ogilvy and Lord and Lady Romsey, kept herself to herself. She had a separate cabin, declined to join the adults for meals and spent her days playing with the children. Knowing her husband's routine, she was unsurprised when she once again overheard Charles speaking on the yacht's telephone to his special friend. 'Why don't you go off with your lady and have an end to it?' she asked him wearily. The princess found this holiday yet another example of royal duplicity and self-serving hypocrisy.

As much as Charles's circle struggled to postpone the evil hour, the net was closing around the prince and his 'other woman'. Throughout the summer of 1992, the *News of the World* received a number of anonymous letters delivered by hand to the security lodge at its office site at Wapping in London's East End. They were addressed to 'Mr Goodwin'—Clive Goodman is the royal correspondent—and detailed the dates and places of meetings between Camilla and Charles in Dorset, Gloucestershire and Wiltshire. Every detail proved to be reliable.

During the same period a hoax letter, on Buckingham Palace writing paper, containing 'information' about the Waleses' private life, was sent to various newspapers. This was followed by a phone call about the memo from a man claiming to be a 'royal insider', who was soon unmasked as the publisher of an eccentric tome about the Princess of Wales. Days later, however, the Duchess of York was at the heart of another plot which this time proved to be non-fiction.

The duchess, her daughters and her 'financial adviser', John Bryan, accompanied by a couple of Scotland Yard detectives, flew secretly in a private plane to the South of France. She and Bryan had taken every precaution to ensure privacy. Yet as they frolicked by the pool in their villa, a photographer captured these intimate moments on film. The resulting pictures, showing Bryan sucking Fergie's toes and kissing her, made headline news around the world. It was devastating, both for her public image and her negotiating position regarding the financial settlement she hoped to obtain from the royal family when she divorced. She and Bryan suspected dirty tricks. She confided her fear to an unsurprised Princess of Wales. Fergie, who had prudently organized a highly placed 'mole' inside the royal system before her departure from royal life, was told: 'You were set up.'

The idea had been to show the duchess, who had earned the unenviable soubriquet 'Freebie Fergie', enjoying another sunshine holiday. However the Palace and the public got rather more than they bargained for. While this may seem unbelievably Machiavellian, both the duchess and the Princess of Wales accepted, and acted upon, this intelligence. Worse was to follow. Publication of the compromising pictures coincided with Fergie's stay at Balmoral. She has since described it as 'the lowest point of my life'—Prince Andrew was so concerned that he called the local doctor—and she only found some solace by talking to the Princess of Wales.

Diana had troubles of her own. Just as negotiations were about to be renewed in August 1992 on the vexed question of the royal separation, she was told that the Sun newspaper was preparing to publish an illicit tape of her conversation with a man, thought to be her friend James Gilbey. The subsequent publication of the so-called Squidgy tape in the Sun under the banner headline 'My life is just torture' was one of the most embarrassing episodes of the princess's royal career. At Balmoral the Queen and Prince Charles discussed the implications of the tape, while at other less grand breakfast tables the public digested the substance of the conversation alleged to have taken place on New Year's Eve 1989 while Diana was staying with the royal family at Sandringham in Norfolk.

Initially there was scepticism about the tape's veracity, especially as Buckingham Palace seemed to suggest it was a hoax. As one newspaper editor observed: 'All it needed was one phone call from Sir Robert Fellowes asking us to calm things down. But nothing happened.' As with Fergie's photos, the timing of publication of the tape was cruel, coming as it did when Diana was at Balmoral, a holiday occasion with the royal family, which, even in normal circumstances, she found such a strain that it often brought on her bulimia.

It emerged that her alleged, racy conversation with

a male admirer, who was speaking from his car phone, was independently taped by two curious radio hams, a retired bank manager and a typist, who both lived within transmission distance of a roadside near Abingdon, Oxfordshire where the calls were made. During the conversation the princess is heard lamenting her isolation inside the royal family, her impossible life with Prince Charles and her criticism of the Duchess of York. She spoke of her fear of becoming pregnant, her anxiety about a clandestine meeting with her admirer and her dreams for the future. 'I'll go out and conquer the world . . . do my bit in the way I know how and leave him behind,' she says, after complaining that her husband made her life 'real, real torture'. Amid the chatter about mutual friends, astrological predictions and fashion—Diana admitted that she dressed another admirer, Army officer James Hewitt 'from head to foot'—the couple discuss the royal family. The princess dismisses Fergie's attempts to use the TV personality, Jimmy Savile, to help her mend her image. She recalls the 'strange look' the Queen Mother fixed upon her during lunch—'It's not hatred, it's sort of interest and pity,' she reflects as she complains about mealtimes with the royal family at Sandringham. 'I was very bad at lunch and I nearly started blubbing. I just felt really sad and empty and thought "bloody hell, after all I've done for this fucking family". . . It is just so desperate. Always being innuendo, the fact that I'm going to do something dramatic because I can't stand the confines of this marriage.' During the conversation the princess, obviously lonely, despondent and neglected, derives much comfort from her besotted admirer who calls her 'darling' fifty-three times and 'Squidgy' or 'Squidge' fourteen times. Their long-distance dalliance, at a time when the princess was only just beginning to fight her eating disorder, bulimia nervosa, and come to terms with her husband's relationship with Camilla Parker Bowles, vividly demonstrates her chronically low self-esteem as well as an embryonic ambition to use her undoubted abilities outside the confines of the royal system.

Diana was 'devastated' by the front-page treatment given to the Squidgy tape, while Gilbey became Britain's most wanted man, hunted day and night by teams of journalists. He spent most of the next couple of weeks in hiding, moving from place to place in the trunks of friends' cars, while Diana tried to put on a brave face in front of the royal family. Her moods swung wildly. 'I ain't going anywhere. I haven't got a single supporter in this family but they are not going to break me,' she told anxious friends, only to confess later: 'If this is the price of public life then it is too high a price to pay.'

While her comments about becoming pregnant were not published until the eve of her visit to Nepal in March 1993, every morning she anxiously waited for news to see if that aspect of the tape was to be published. She knew full well that Prince Charles, whom she described as 'cockahoop' following the tape's publication, and his circle were anxious that a full transcript of her conversation was printed. They felt it helped to even the score. As one of Charles's aristocratic friends told a Sun newspaper executive: 'If News International (owners of the Sun) do not say that Diana is an adulteress then they will lose all credibility.' Her sense of isolation in this hostile climate was complete. A friend who consoled her during this time recalled:

She is at the lowest ebb for years. Her self-confidence is destroyed. Diana will crumble if she doesn't get the support she deserves and if they publish the quotes about the pregnancy she will leave. In fact she is on the verge of packing her bags tonight.

Diana's circle was genuinely divided about her best course of action. Should she sit out the storm, damaged but still fighting, or should she leave the fray for the sake of her peace of mind? One close friend told her: 'If you don't go they will destroy you. If your white wedding dress is now shown to be ivory that is no bad thing. The age of innocence is over for the monarchy and ourselves.' As the storm began to subside, the princess recovered a little of her nerve, the customary Spencer steel surfacing from time to time. She told her circle: 'I've had two weeks' bad publicity in eleven years. If you tell me in two months that it's going against me then I'll believe it. It's a tough business but I'm not giving up. This whole campaign has been run on fantasy and fabrication.' The head of the Royal Protection Squad sent a memo to every member of the royal family banning them from using mobile phones for 'sensitive' calls, a classic case of shutting the stable door after the horse has bolted.

As the princess licked her wounds she received a telephone call, this time on a secure line, which made her blood run cold. She was told that Captain James Hewitt, upon whom she had lavished so much generosity, was about to sell his story to a tabloid. Diana was appalled. She could handle the backstabbing from Charles's circle, but betrayal from her own side was unforgivable. 'I find it very hard to believe,' she said. Quite by chance Hewitt phoned the princess just a few hours after she had digested the warning call. When she asked him about his intentions, Hewitt was uncharacteristically evasive. Eventually he denied the allegation. It wasn't until nearly two years later that he decided to go public about his five-year friendship with the princess. Perversely Prince Charles's supporters believed that Hewitt was simply Diana's stalking-horse, and that his story would merely be another 'voice' putting her side of things: one more stepping-stone on the way out of the royal family.

At the same time, Diana was aware that the locked safe at the offices of the *News of the World* already contained a controversial story about her relationship with Hewitt as revealed by his disaffected valet, Lance-Corporal Malcolm Leete. Within days of her telephone interview with Hewitt, Leete's story chronicling the early-morning riding lessons featuring the princess and the dashing major at Combermere Barracks, Windsor was front-page news. According to Leete, the couple became closer and closer, Diana showing her appreciation for Hewitt's professional help in the form of expensive presents, including a diamond-studded tiepin and gold and silver clock from the royal jeweller, Asprey. At first Hewitt sued for libel but later rescinded his suit arguing that he couldn't afford to continue the legal battle.

This fresh personal crisis could hardly have come at a less propitious moment. Diana knew that she would be on the defensive during future negotiations. Ever ready to defer to her sovereign, she had several conversations with the Queen, who finally convinced Diana that she should accompany her husband on the official visit to South Korea, scheduled for November. The instability of their marriage had meant that the prince's deputy private secretary, Peter Westmacott, had flown out to the Far East with instructions to arrange two itineraries; one to include the princess and one with the prince alone. Diana, although in no mood to argue, believed that the media focus on their marriage would detract from the visit itself.

Ultimately, the princess is always loyal to the Crown and she was aware that the Queen had her own difficulties in a year she would later describe as her *annus horribilis*; her solicitor, Sir Matthew Farrer, was deep in negotiations with Downing Street over secret proposals to pay income tax; numerous senior Church figures were castigating the royal family for not providing a healthy example of family life; and opinion polls revealed the general public's growing disaffection with the monarchy. A timely reminder of what being royal entails was provided by Prince Michael of Kent, who publicly warned his relations: 'If you have privilege, which in my case came from birth, you have no option but to accept some kind of obligation. You can't have all the perks without pulling your own weight.' The Prime Minister, John Major, tacitly acknowledged the crisis facing the House of Windsor when he described the monarchy as 'entrenched, enduring and valuable' as he set off to see the Queen at Balmoral for his traditional visit.

It was against this background of public and private disquiet that, in the autumn of 1992, the Princess of Wales embarked on a series of meetings with her private secretary, Patrick Jephson, and her lawyer, Paul Butner, to discuss an official separation from her husband and her royal future. She dismissed newspaper headlines saying that she was demanding her own palace as 'ridiculous speculation', and told anyone who would listen: 'All I want is for Charles to leave Kensington Palace.' This was her short-term objective now that the fracture in the fairytale royal marriage was obvious to all. Those involved with the delicate negotiations recall her evident vulnerability. 'She was terrified that the family were going to take the children away and drive her into exile,' recalls an adviser. 'It was her greatest anxiety and she was prepared to give up everything, do anything to keep the boys.' Diana needed no reminding about her own parents' divorce, which had ended in an acrimonious court case where her mother, Frances Shand Kydd, lost custody of her four children to Diana's father, Earl Spencer.

Meetings between the Waleses to discuss the issues involved in a formal separation were invariably emotional and highly strung, ending, and sometimes starting, with slammed doors, raised voices and moist eyes. 'They yelled at each other as is the way in messy divorces,' recalls one participant in the meetings. Lord Goodman, a venerable legal figure, was brought in to arbitrate on the constitutional questions raised by the prospect of a formal separation. At various stages the Prime Minister was consulted and asked if a separation would have an effect on the governance of the country. He indicated that it would have none.

For the most part the children, the couple's homes and their offices formed the nucleus of discussion. At the same time as asking Charles to leave Kensington Palace, Diana also wanted to divorce her office staff from his, which were both based at St James's Palace, and move her employees to quarters at Buckingham Palace. This demand was unacceptable to Charles. He was unwilling to pack his bags, saw no reason to split their administrative staff and was firm about the future of the children. An adviser to the prince recalls: 'The prince was reluctant to go down the road of a formal separation and divorce, not only for the sake of the children but also because of the constitutional mess which would arise from that. Basically, he wanted things to continue as they were but for them to live apart.' As his staff will testify, one of his favourite phrases is 'anything for the quiet life'.

The man, who from birth had lived on the autopilot of duty and an almost other-worldly obligation to the nation, now had to confront the wretched state of his marriage and his impossible relationship with his wife, which had troubled him long before the difficult summer of 1992. As one of his advisers told me:

Years before your book came out the prince was suffering agonies with his marriage. Here was a man who likes a calm, ordered existence, painting on the beach or walking on the hills. He went through mental anguish every time he met her because he experienced at first-hand the slamming of doors, the threats, the shouting, the stamping of feet, the sheer unreasonableness of her behaviour. When he appeared with her in public his stomach would be permanently knotted with tension. He dreaded that she would cause a scene.

At one meeting where the princess talked about 'my children', her husband coolly pointed out that she had the wrong idea, these were the children of the future king. Diana played her ace. Her despair with the royal system was such that she threatened Prince Charles that she would take her children and live abroad, making a new life in Australia. At first her proposal was treated with mockery. Then they began to take it seriously. For Prince Charles and the royal family, who now regarded Diana as 'out of control', it was their worst nightmare come true. At a council of war Charles's advisers, quoting the precedent of the Duke of Windsor, who rarely returned to Britain following his abdication, argued that the princess was such a danger to the monarchy that she should be encouraged to live in Australia alone, effectively in exile. Diana's ace was matched.

The notion of life without her children was simply appalling. She was reminded very forcibly that her children were the immediate heirs to the throne and as such had to be raised inside the royal court in order to give them the experience to perform their royal duties. Not only was she faced with the stern moral prerogatives of their royal heritage, but she was also made chillingly aware of the stark legal realities underlying her predicament. Laws which apply exclusively to the royal family effectively deny a royal mother any real say in the upbringing of her children. In bald terms, the Princess of Wales, universally admired as a caring mother, has fewer rights over her children than a divorcée raising a family in a tenement. Absurd as it may seem, technically the law can prevent her from being the mother she wants to be. Her ace was trumped.

The brown leather-bound volumes of *Halsbury's Statutes* reveal that, under common law, the sovereign has the right to control the care and education of her immediate family including her grandchildren. This was the opinion of ten out of twelve judges when

George I consulted them in 1717 during a wrangle with his son, George, Prince of Wales, over the education of his grandson, Prince Frederick. It is a judgment which has gone unchallenged for nearly three centuries. As Diana's lawyer warned, if she wanted to take on the Queen it would be no contest. She would lose. If it was any consolation, so would Prince Charles. The judgment, known as The Grand Question, lays down that the sovereign has the right of supervision of the heirs presumptive, in this case Princes William and Harry, even during their parents' lifetime.

While the Queen has the final say over the custody and upbringing of the young princes, all Diana can do is exercise her discretion and negotiate. Indeed, the Queen, although by no means a meddler, used this ultimate sanction when the princess planned for herself and her sons to go skiing in Lech, Austria, late in March 1994, without armed bodyguards. Diana made the decision knowing full well that the paparazzi would be out in force, but she would not back down, even at the request of senior officers from the Royal Protection Squad. As a last resort the matter was referred to the Queen, and it was only at the sovereign's express insistence that Diana allowed bodyguards to shadow her boys. Even then, on the night before they were due to fly to Zurich, she changed her mind and barred the royal minders. Too late. With ill-concealed grace Diana allowed her royal shadows to join her party while making it clear that they were only to guard the boys and not interfere with her own holiday.

Much has been made of Diana's heartache when her boys stay with their father and the rest of the royal family at traditional occasions such as Christmas at Sandringham and Easter at Windsor Castle. While it is sensible that the heir and the 'spare' to the throne understand their duties and responsibilities inside the Court, the princess and her legal advisers realize that ultimately they are powerless against the Queen and the Prince of Wales on this issue. Diana acknowledged as much in her 'Time and Space' speech in December 1993, where she announced her withdrawal from public life. 'My first priority will continue to be our children, William and Harry, who deserve as much love, care and attention as I am able to give, as well as an appreciation of the tradition into which they were born.'

While the Princess of Wales had only one battle to fight, her husband faced a war on two fronts—Diana and Camilla. Camilla was as exasperated as the princess about his continual vacillation. What promises he had made, what dreams of the future they had planned only Charles and Camilla know. None the less the princess gleefully told her friends of a conversation between her husband and his erstwhile girlfriend where she told him: 'You never do anything you say. When are you going to make your mind up?' As Diana told her friends: 'I didn't realize that she is pushing for exactly the same as me.' It gave Diana a frisson of satisfaction, especially after a televised service of commemoration at Westminster Abbey showed all three of them in attendance. 'The nerve of the woman,' she indignantly told her friends.

During that tense autumn of 1992, the two royal camps seized upon every scrap of news, hearsay and rumour. For a time the princess was convinced that Andrew Parker Bowles was resolved upon a divorce, citing her husband as the other party in his petition. This would have sealed Diana's triumph, at once ridding herself of her husband, vanquishing her rival and demonstrating to the world that she was blameless in the breakdown of her marriage. Her feelings of triumph were short-lived. No sooner had the story been absorbed than Diana was telling her circle that Buckingham Palace had put intense pressure on the Parker Bowleses not to rock the royal boat. In fact, Diana's instincts proved unerring. The Parker Bowleses, who divorced in January 1995, cited February 1992 as the date when their marriage had irretrievably broken down. For three years they went through the motions of a marriage while in reality leading separate lives.

Still the steady drizzle of pro-Charles stories continued. It emerged that he had received a rapturous reception from his staff at Highgrove when he hosted a party; that Diana had banned the boys from accompanying their father on a visit to a new children's museum in Halifax; and that he had commissioned the broadcaster, Jonathan Dimbleby, to write his biography, described as the 'complete riposte' to

Diana, Her True Story, to coincide with the twenty-fifth anniversary of his investiture. The image of a loyal employer, a loving if thwarted father, and a misunderstood public figure, who was there for the duration was now beginning to emerge. As the preparations were completed for the joint visit to Korea, Prince Charles's private secretary briefed several newspaper editors, including Sir Nicholas Lloyd of the *Daily Express,* that this would be the 'togetherness tour'. 'She's got her sparkle back—maybe she's in love,' opined one newspaper.

It was a short-lived bandwagon. The princess was in no mood to continue with the hollow hypocrisy now that separation negotiations had reached a critical stage. She intended to signal her distance from her husband but, as with the Trooping the Colour ceremony in June, to demonstrate her allegiance to the Crown. 'It is the grown-up thing to do,' she remarked. A friend who discussed her plans before she set off on what would be her last tour with Prince Charles recalled: 'She was determined to try and show the world what was really going on. Diana had come so far she was in no mood to be blown off course by a silly charade.' Headlines like 'The Glums' and 'How much longer can this tragedy go on?' ensured that her ploy was successful. As one commentator remarked: 'On the tarmac yesterday in Seoul, the dewy-eyed mask of put-upon innocence conveyed a familiar message: "I am so unhappy. I am being treated so badly."' Such was Diana's sense of despair that on one occasion she phoned the Duchess of York from

Seoul telling her plaintively: 'I've got to get out of here.'

The tour was also dogged by exaggerated reports of the contents of the paperback version of *Diana, Her True Story*, which briefly mentioned the angry letters Diana had received from Prince Philip. By the time the embroidered story appeared in the tabloids, the innocent reader could be forgiven for thinking that Prince Philip had put pen to paper with Fleet Street's finest at his elbow. It led to a brief public statement by Diana, where she explained her relationship with the Queen and the Duke of Edinburgh. 'The suggestion that they have been anything other than sympathetic and supportive is untrue and particularly hurtful,' she said. Ideally, the princess would have only included the Queen's name but, given the circumstances of the reports, that was impossible. At the same time, she hoped that by omitting mention of Prince Charles she was preparing the public for their separation. She dropped other hints. During a visit to Paris she was in high spirits after hearing from her lawyer that at last Prince Charles had agreed to leave Kensington Palace. She told the veteran photographer, Arthur Edwards, cryptically: 'It's time to spread my wings.'

Just hours before the announcement of the official separation in the House of Commons on 9 December 1992, Diana had her own domestic crisis to deal with. As Buckingham Palace and Downing Street synchronized the timing of the news, the princess's mind was on other matters. An early-morning telephone call from her mother, Frances Shand Kydd, greatly disturbed her. She had always had a turbulent relationship with her mother, veering from times of genuine closeness to long periods of silence, but this conversation was one of the most emotionally trying of her life. Her mother's tone was self-pitying, tearfully hysterical and destructive. Unlucky in love—she had seen two marriages end in divorce—Diana's mother was in the depths of despair following the collapse of a third serious relationship. Diana laid aside her own problems and, using all of her counselling skills, managed to calm her mother down and talk her out of her melancholy. It was an added emotional burden to bear at a time of unprecedented stress.

There were more tears to dry when she visited her boys, Princes William and Harry, at Ludgrove School in Berkshire to break the news of the separation. The boys were ushered into headmaster Gerald Barber's private rooms and there, with the headmaster's wife Jane by her side, the princess explained the new arrangements in their lives. Prince William, then aged ten, burst into floods of tears while Prince Harry, two years his junior, seemed both nonplussed and indifferent. Their reactions were as much to do with their ages—older children are more deeply affected by parental disturbance—as their characters. Harry, extrovert, impish yet thoughtful, is a perfect foil for his shy, rather formal elder brother. Of the two, it is William who is drawn to his mother—'I want to be a policeman so that I can look after you, mummy,' he once said. During that tearful encounter she steadfastly refrained from mentioning the name of the woman who had cast a long shadow over her marriage and, to her mind, was the incubus who had destroyed it.

Camilla Parker Bowles was not, nor never will be, used by Diana as a reason for the breakdown of her marriage—at least as far as the children are concerned. Discussions with her own divorced girlfriends had made her acutely aware of the distress caused to children when 'the other woman' was given as a reason for the collapse of the marriage. At that time the princess was not sure if Charles would go off and marry his other love and, whatever her own feelings, maternal common sense told her not to jeopardize her children's possible relationship with their future stepmother. For the princess, her boys came first—whatever the cost. This altruism was sorely tested when the Parker Bowleses divorced and the prospect of Queen Camilla became a tantalizing reality. Diana told friends that she would prefer Tiggy Legge-Bourke as a stepmother to the children, rather than her long-time love rival. That was in the future. Before she left Ludgrove, Diana ensured that the school would prevent William and Harry reading the newspapers.

While she too followed her own advice and ignored the front-page headlines, she was alert to an aspect of Prime Minister John Major's statement, which had created much debate. He told disbelieving Members of Parliament: 'There is no reason why the Princess of Wales should not be crowned Queen in due course.' Lord Blake, the constitutional historian, speaking at the behest of the Palace, added later that the Prime Minister was merely quoting the existing legal position. Even so, it created consternation inside and outside Parliament. Tory MP John Bowis expressed most people's views: 'You couldn't conceivably have two carriage processions coming from different parts of London to Westminster Abbey for the coronation and then going separate ways. They have to arrive together or I'm afraid there has to be a skipping of a generation.' As debate raged about the rights and wrongs of crowning William the next king, a weary Princess of Wales described Major's comments as 'unhelpful.' Indeed to underline his commitment to the throne following the separation in December, Prince Charles allowed his closest advisers to disseminate a story stating that he had no intention of remarrying and pledging his allegiance to the Crown. An adviser argued: 'He does not want to go down in history as Charles the Divorced.' Once again sage legal counsel was sought. Lord Goodman advised that a divorced king would be acceptable to the country but a twice-married sovereign would not.

Diana knew instinctively from the moment Prince Charles had asked her to marry him in the nursery at Windsor Castle that she would never be Queen. 'A voice inside me said: "You won't be Queen but you will have a tough role." ' The passage of the years has merely confirmed that early instinct.

As 1992 drew to a close, Diana was emotionally exhausted and physically drained. 'I simply haven't got anything left to give,' she said to friends. As her

71

former astrologer, Penny Thornton, commented: 'This time is an enormous test of the health of a woman who is extremely vulnerable to emotional pressures. In many ways it is unfair. If ever she needed spiritual and therapeutic guidance, it's now.' Yet in the days before the relative peace and privacy of Christmas with her brother at Althorp in Northamptonshire, she still had to steel herself for numerous high-profile engagements and speeches. She did, however, write to Princess Anne politely declining an invitation to her wedding to Commander Timothy Laurence, a former equerry to the Queen, on the grounds that her presence would take away attention from her big day.

The events of the Queen's *annus horribilis*—the separations of the Yorks and Waleses, the topless photos of Fergie, the various intimate tapes of royal conversations, the sovereign's decision to pay income tax and pare down the Civil List—had effectively ended the royal fairytale. The year 1992 saw the collision of mythology and reality, a year when unadorned facts triumphed over homely fiction. 'The symbolism of the fire at Windsor Castle was not lost on anyone inside the family,' Diana told her friends.

It was the royal family's image as the 'perfect' family that inevitably took the severest blow. It was no longer possible, as it had been in previous generations, to hide the fact that the royals are fallible human beings. The shattering of the myth was welcomed, significantly by the marriage-guidance charity Relate, whose patron was the Princess of Wales. Six days after her separation from Prince Charles, Relate director David French said in a speech:

No longer should we expect a public opinion which will be hood-winked by the powerful icons of the two-plus-two, gleaming teeth and never-a-row families of TV commercials or by the dishonest pretence that our public figures should attain a level of domestic perfection to which we would never aspire ourselves. The public mood in this country is now much more willing to accept that families of various shapes can and do function well—some with one parent, some with two.

For too many years Diana had been an unwilling party to the humbug surrounding her life inside the royal family. As one of Diana's closest confidantes remarked: 'She feels now that there is nothing more to hide. It is all out in the open. There is no need to go on lying or hiding from the truth. That fact alone has given her much strength in the turmoil of the last few months.' For years both Diana and Fergie had lived and breathed the myth of serene royal marriages and a benign monarchy. It very nearly destroyed them both, mentally and physically. 'Last year we helped save a life, I truly believe that,' said one of Diana's coterie, privately defending her decision to speak about Diana's lonely hell inside the royal family.

Now, at last, the princess was ready to cast off the shackles of a desperately unhappy marriage. A new life beckoned, a freer existence, which only a year before would have seemed like an impossible dream. A fresh start alone, but a life still to be lived inside the royal family and the royal system she had come to despise and distrust. It was an uneasy compromise and it was not long before Diana chafed once more at the bars of her gilded cage. As she told her friends: 'I have contracted, I've agreed to pay the piper for now. The fun is to come, maybe in two or three years.

'I'm learning to be patient.'

3

'My Friend, Mr Gorilla'

THE FIRST DECISION DIANA MADE was to throw out
the mahogany double bed she had slept in at Kensington Palace since her marriage eleven years before. Then she had the bedroom painted, changed
the locks and her private telephone number. But she
kept 'Mr Gorilla', a large stuffed animal, who lolled
against one of the cream bedroom walls. 'He keeps
an eye on me,' she says with a smile. She kept too the
menagerie of cuddly animals collected from her
childhood. They live on the sofa at the foot of the
bed, while her battered but much-loved teddy takes
pride of place on her pillow. Her zoo of comforting
creatures—surprising, as she has no real pets—was
much expanded when removal vans carrying her

trinkets and keepsakes from Highgrove arrived. Diana's group of frogs soon squeezed on to her already cluttered bedroom table to join other pottery animals and daintily decorated Crummel boxes. Her diving cup from West Heath school found its place among the bottles of aromatherapy oils, bath essences, talcs and perfumes in her modest marble en-suite bathroom. As she carefully puts on her make-up in front of the huge theatrical bathroom mirror, the princess looks at her trophy and is reminded of happier, more innocent days.

For many years there had been little laughter and even fewer smiles at apartments eight and nine, which the Prince and Princess of Wales had made their London home. 'I feel I have died in that house many, many times,' Diana has told friends. Visitors were quick to sense the cheerless atmosphere— words like 'dead energy', 'gloomy' and 'tense' sprang to mind. Even Diana's bedroom was suffused by an air of sadness. 'I can imagine her lying in bed at night cuddling her teddy and crying,' observed a former member of staff, commenting on this little girl's bedroom, populated by staring animals.

In the months following the separation, frequent callers began to notice a change. The staff seemed friendlier, less formal, the atmosphere lighter and more relaxed. 'There was a lot more banter and laughter, not so much creeping around,' notes a friend. 'Even the cleaners say hello.' This is a change from the days when they had to hide in cupboards when royalty was around. During the winter of 1992 there was much toing and froing between Highgrove, St James's Palace and Kensington Palace. The painting of a kilted Prince Charles which had hung in the entrance hall of Kensington Palace was packed up, as were his paintings and prints of hunting, shooting and ceremonial scenes. His heavy mahogany desk, his library containing, among others, books inscribed by Winston Churchill and Laurens van der Post, and other memorabilia were carefully carted away while Diana was on holiday in the Caribbean with Princes William and Harry.

In a secret, carefully planned night operation, his military and ceremonial uniforms were covered in plastic, hung on metal rails, similar to those used in clothing stores, and ferried to St James's Palace, where they were wheeled across the courtyard into the prince's new apartments. 'It was an undignified and very sad finale to the fairytale,' according to one Palace official. At the same time a convoy of removal vans headed east, carrying Diana's personal possessions from Highgrove; she had spent a desultory weekend wandering through her former home, pointing out to staff the things she wanted. Diana's prints by Raoul Dufy, watercolours by Sir Hugh Casson and a pencil sketch of her grandfather, the 7th Earl Spencer, by Adrian Beach, were swapped for Charles's polo prints, silver-framed family photographs and rich leather-bound books on military campaigns. The couple, who had received an Aladdin's Cave of gifts during their marriage valued at £10 million, coolly consigned unwanted gifts and possessions to the flames. A bonfire of their vanities, including a chess set, Charles-and-Diana headed notepaper, ornamental figures and other bric-a-brac, was made in the grounds of Highgrove. It was, said an official, part of a clear out; valuable items were put in store at Windsor Castle or given to charity. A silver model of HMS *Bronington*, Prince Charles's only Navy command, escaped the purge. It remains in the downstairs waiting room at Kensington Palace, one of the few reminders of his tenure in the elegant royal condominium which is also home to Princess Margaret, Prince and Princess Michael of Kent, Princess Alice and the Duke and Duchess of Gloucester.

Diana was not so fortunate. Over the next few months every sign that she had ever lived at Highgrove was systematically wiped away. Charles hired a local designer, Robert Kime, to redecorate Highgrove and his new home at St James's Palace, which was formerly occupied by the Lord Chamberlain, the Earl of Airlie. When Prince Edward and his girlfriend Sophie Rhys-Jones visited Charles's country home, she could not help noticing that, among the scores of family photographs and portraits, there was not one picture of his estranged wife.

Nor for that matter were there any of Charles in Princess Diana's first-floor private sitting room at Kensington Palace. 'They were probably shredded years ago,' said a friend. That room throughout Diana's marriage was, in Diana's words, 'my retreat, my empire and my nest', and gives a fascinating 'Through the Keyhole' glimpse into her character, moods and interests. The sound of loud music, and the scent of freesias, her favourite flowers, and white Casablanca lilies greet visitors. Songs from musicals like *Phantom of the Opera* and *Les Misérables* are favourites, as is the *Chariots of Fire* composer, Vangelis. Most frequently though, she relaxes to the strains of choral or church music by Bach, Handel and Mozart. The jasmine-scented candles burning by the marble fireplace enhance the mood of peace and soothe her nerves.

Her sitting room is a shrine to the two men in her life, Princes William and Harry. In front of the fireplace is a five-foot leather rhino cushion for them to lie on as they watch television, while on every conceivable surface there are wooden and silver-framed photographs of them go-carting, in tanks, on horseback, cycling, fishing, on police bikes or in school uniform. Five black-and-white Patrick Demarchelier photographs of the boys, which decorate the nursery, are her favourites.

Framed photographs of her late father, Earl Spencer, sisters Jane and Sarah, and her brother Charles adorn the sitting-room mantelpiece. There are also snaps in this gallery of the princess herself: a signed black-and-white photograph of her dancing with the film director Richard Attenborough, another with singer Elton John, a third with Liza Minnelli, and other privately taken pictures of the princess imitating Audrey Hepburn in outfits from the film *Breakfast at Tiffany's*. Dresser drawers are stuffed with pictures and albums; one light-hearted snap shows her as a teenager 'mooning' for the camera with the word 'Oops' written underneath.

When the mood takes her she will show close friends a video she made with her former dance teacher, Anne Miller, performing a routine to the music from the film *Top Gun* and *Phantom of the Opera*. Signed pairs of ballet shoes hang behind the door and from a table. Dance paintings by her favourite artist, American, Robert Heindel, decorate the walls. (She went for a secret early-morning viewing of his latest work, when it was displayed in an Oxford Street department store.) As a child, she would join other schoolgirls waiting outside the stage door of the Royal Opera House hoping to get an autograph from a favourite dancer. The girl who famously grew too tall to be a ballerina is still fascinated by the movement and athleticism of this most graceful of arts. Her technical knowledge of dance is considerable and she often makes time to watch dancers in rehearsal, celebrating their triumphs and consoling them in their failures. 'At least you have been noticed,' she said to the director of the Royal Ballet, Anthony Dowell, after a series of unfavourable reviews.

Since her marriage, the princess has developed a keen interest in psychology and, in particular, women's role in the world. Feminists who once dismissed her as 'too sweet, too neat, and too obedient' would be surprised at titles like *Women and Power* by Nancy Klein or *The Triumph of the Western Mind*, as well as books on healing and the power of positive-thinking. Her current interest in Islamic philosophy and culture was inspired by her friend, Oliver Hoare: 'I've got 101 books I want to read, I'm gripped by them,' Diana says.

She was absorbed in Brian Keenan's An Evil Cradling, a chillingly candid account of his life as a hostage in Beirut, and uplifted by Jill Morrell's part in Some Other Rainbow, where she tells of her long struggle for the release of her hostage boyfriend, John McCarthy. Diana's morbid fear of closed spaces and sense of imprisonment within the royal system gave the books a special resonance. Indeed, a constant reminder of the caution and confinement of her world is the grey, battery-powered shredding machine, which sits uneasily above a wastepaper bin by the desk in her sitting room. Like hostages and their captors, Diana has a love-hate relationship with her home in Kensington Palace. It represents so much accumulated misery and heartache for her, and yet, as she tells friends, 'I feel secure here.' Her sitting room, crowded with comforting groups of pottery animals, photo frames, enamel boxes and figurines, gives the impression of a woman trying to protect herself from the incursions of the outside world. 'It is like an old lady's room, packed to the gunwales with knick-knacks,' observes a girlfriend. 'It must be a nightmare to dust and a minefield for the children. You can hardly move.' Another close friend explains the mentality behind this profusion. 'It's very common for people coming from a broken home to want material possessions around them. They are building their own nests.'

Diana's gentle, occasionally self-deprecating, sense of humour does lighten the general air of claustrophobia. Examples literally litter the sitting room. On every chair are silk cushions embroidered with humorous motifs such as: 'Good girls go to heaven, bad girls go everywhere', 'You have to kiss a lot of frogs before you find a prince' and 'I feel sorry for people who don't drink because when they wake up in the morning that is the best they are going to feel all day.' Her bathroom and lavatory are decorated with newspaper cartoons depicting Prince Charles talking to his plants, and their visit to the Pope in the Vatican; these give a glimpse of what tickles her funny bone.

Her dry wit—a joke she enjoys is to describe to visitors the logistics of transporting bread all the way from Highgrove to end up as tiny pieces of toast at her dining table—often impresses callers granted thirty-minute audiences in the formal drawing room. The variety of visitors reveals the wide spectrum of her interests. Mike Whitlam of the Red Cross and Sandra Horley of Refuge, the battered women's charity, are regulars, but in any one week she could be seeing a hospice matron, a professor studying spinal injuries, commanding officers from her regiments, the film director David Puttnam or even taking tea with the teenage, pop heart-throbs, Take That. A fortunate few are invited to stay for lunch in the next-door dining room. The days when she felt so helpless that she was embarrassed to invite friends for lunch are fast receding. She is now an accomplished hostess, able to tell a risqué joke, while using the bell under her place setting to summon her butler, Paul Burrell. Visitors disagree with the assessment of the Queen's former private secretary, Lord Charteris, that she has 'little small talk'. Visitors describe lunches as 'chatty and informal' and the food, prepared by chef Mervyn Wycherley, as light and imaginative. Small decorative changes since the separation have been noticed; the walls have been repainted, terracotta pots are filled with arrangements of mosses and twigs, and the stark military and architectural paintings have been replaced with gentle landscapes. While the prevailing mood is inevitably more feminine, Diana has never quite made up her mind to follow her initial impulse and completely redecorate her house.

For months following the separation she vacillated between wanting to stay at Kensington Palace and feeling she would like to move into a country home of her own. Her procrastination illuminates much about her position inside the royal family. Nearly two years before the split she had actively discussed the possibility of buying her own country home. The feeling of living inside an open prison at Kensington Palace with the constant surveillance from staff and police gnawed at her spirit. Highgrove she found equally dispiriting. It was Charles's domain; the house where Camilla was queen. She longed to break free and yet realized that if she did buy a house it would be interpreted that she was walking out on her marriage. A friend recalls: 'She would in effect be saying it's all over. She would be seen to be the one making the break and so she would have been blamed for ending the marriage. One thing which concerns her above all else is a deep fear of censure and condemnation. So, as ever, she drew back.'

Once the separation was announced, Diana looked again at the possibility of moving. In the spring of 1993, she became increasingly unhappy with having to live in Kensington Palace. She very rarely spends weekends away with friends, other than Julia and Michael Samuel, in their beautiful home in Berkshire, or at the country retreat of Lord and Lady Palumbo. When she returns to Kensington Palace she feels a familiar sinking feeling. 'I wake up on Sunday morning and I dread going back,' she told friends. 'It's like returning to prison.' Her feelings of being hemmed in and watched by the security cameras and police merely intensified her need to find her own private place. However other considerations came into play. She was concerned that if she was seen to be spending a small fortune on her own house it would not go down well with the public nor would it sit easily with Prince Charles's camp or Buckingham Palace courtiers. She felt, probably correctly, that there would be hostile debate inside and outside the Palace about the security costs involved in protecting a Princess of Wales, who was now, after all, only an extra on the fringe of the royal family. Just as she had given up a red Mercedes sports car in the months before the separation because she didn't want to be seen as a spendthrift, so she feared that the public might be critical if the taxpayer had to fork out thousands of pounds on security measures.

Frustrated by life in London, reluctant to buy her own place, the princess was 'excited and delighted' when, in April 1993, her brother, Earl Spencer, offered her a house on the estate at Althorp. 'At long last I can make a cosy nest of my own,' she told friends, filled with enthusiasm at the idea of decorating and designing her own place. For the first time she would truly be able to express herself without having to look over her shoulder or be reminded of sad events. Her brother's offer of the Garden House, a four-bedroomed property near to Althorp House, also neatly sidestepped the problem of seeming to be extravagant. She contacted Dudley Poplak, the South African–born designer and family friend who had organized the interior decoration of Kensington Palace. Anxious to move in before the school summer holiday, the princess brought Poplak and the boys to look around the house. After a picnic lunch in the gardens, the boys were free to roam around the grounds while their mother discussed colour schemes, fabrics and wallpapers—pale blues and yellows were provisionally chosen. Above all else she wanted to make her new home 'cosy'. It was her constant refrain as the exciting vista of a new life opened up before her. The Garden House had an added bonus. It was not overlooked by any of the buildings on the estate, giving her total privacy. Best of all, the ubiquitous armed bodyguard would not have to intrude upon her new home as there was a small house close by in which he could be based. Her detectives, Ken Wharfe and Peter Brown, also visited the property, taking instant photographs, and they discussed possible sites for surveillance equipment.

Just three weeks later Diana's brave new world collapsed around her. Earl Spencer telephoned her and said that he no longer felt comfortable with the idea. He argued that the extra police presence, the inevitable cameras and other surveillance—initially the local police insisted on a team of four machine-gun-carrying officers plus sniffer dogs—would involve unacceptable levels of intrusion. With Althorp House also open to the public, her presence would further add to the difficulties of running a stately home and, as a result, various restrictions would have to be placed on her freedom of movement. She was stunned, for once absolutely lost for words. After she recovered her composure she wrote her brother a long letter arguing her case and expressing her extreme disappointment. It was returned unopened. She sent a second asking him to reconsider. No reply was forthcoming. While Earl Spencer had a perfectly valid argument, for Diana it represented much more than simply the loss of a house. Her 'cosy nest' had been a challenge and a new beginning. The Garden House had literally been the home of her dreams. For several months there was a coolness between the princess and her brother.

The issue of the house symbolized a turbulent period between the princess and the rest of the Spencer clan. Already on the outskirts of the royal family, the princess endured a 'tricky' period with her own flesh and blood. The history of her parents' divorce and the former Earl Spencer's subsequent remarriage to Raine, Countess Spencer, had left the family bitter and divided. Diana's grandmother Ruth, Lady Fermoy, the Queen Mother's lady-in-waiting, had never been forgiven by the princess for her decision to give evidence against her own daughter, Frances Shand Kydd, during the hurtful divorce case. Diana had never trusted her grandmother, on one occasion literally pushing her out of the front door of Kensington Palace after a furious altercation. It was no surprise then that, when Charles and Diana separated, Lady Fermoy did not side with her own kith and kin. Diana remembers with some rancour: 'My grandmother tried to lacerate me in any way she could. She fed the royal family with hideous comments about my mother, so whenever I mention her name the royal family come down on me like a ton of bricks. Mummy came across very badly because grandmother did a real hatchet job.'

So it was with surprise approaching astonishment that the family heard of two visits Diana made to see Lady Fermoy at her Eaton Square apartment in June 1993, just three weeks before her grandmother's death. Rather than allowing her feelings of resentment to simmer for more years, the princess decided to confront the woman who had hurt her so badly. It was an understandably frosty encounter, Lady Fermoy visibly taken aback by Diana's courageous decision to raise the problem which had driven them apart, rather than, as is the royal way, to engage in meaningless small talk while the real issues remain

unspoken. Diana explained that while she appreciated her grandmother's loyalty to Prince Charles, she
wanted her to know just how difficult that decision
had made her own life. Visibly shaken by Diana's
emotional and frank admission, Lady Fermoy found it
hard to find words to express her own feelings. While
it would be an exaggeration to say that there was a
reconciliation between these warring relations,
Diana's decision to clear the air did lead to a truce.
When her grandmother died, the princess remarked
that she was glad that they had been able to discuss
their differences. 'The more honest you are, the better
you feel,' she said.

Her refreshing openness and willingness to build
bridges was both a sign of her growing maturity and
determination to lay the ghosts of her past to rest as
she tried to build a new life. This new-found resolve
was at the heart of her emotional reconciliation with
her stepmother, Raine Spencer. It was no secret that
Diana, her sisters and brother had little love for the
woman they called 'Acid Raine'. Stories that the
furious princess once pushed her down a flight of
stairs, enjoyed a shouting match with the daughter of
novelist Barbara Cartland at her brother's wedding,
and giggled at sneering accounts of her subsequent
marriage to French aristocrat, Count Jean François de
Chambrun, were part of Spencer family folk lore—
and made lurid newspaper headlines. When her father, Earl Spencer, died, the princess could have been
excused for consigning Raine to the dustbin of her
life, but she chose not to do so, inviting Raine and her

French husband to lunch. It was an emotional encounter. The talk was of the past, reminiscing about the life of the late Earl Spencer. When the princess thanked Raine for loving her father, in sickness and in health, Raine's famous composure cracked and she burst into tears. That meeting, in May 1993, was a turning point in their relationship. Their frequent meetings since, often dining at Claridge's Hotel, have been frostily received by the rest of the Spencers. On one occasion her mother, Frances Shand Kydd, angrily confronted the princess and demanded to know what on earth she was playing at. Diana explained that before her father died, he had asked her to watch over Raine. It was a promise she intended to keep. She pointed out that as she had hated Raine most and yet had been able to forgive and forget, then so should the rest of the family.

Diana's success in clearing away the emotional brushwood of the past left her free to begin laying the foundations of a new life. A new home was the keystone of her dream. The collapse of that ambition dealt her a grievous blow, coming at a time when her royal life seemed bleaker than ever. Her hopes dashed, the princess spent many months licking her wounds, tolerating but not enjoying life at Kensington Palace. When she announced her decision to withdraw from public life a year after the separation, she also decided that it would be prudent to leave her palace home. She told the Queen: 'I will be out in six months', sensitive to any suggestion that she was enjoying a 'grace and favour' home from the sovereign without reciprocating with work for the monarchy. Diana resolved to find a new home for herself and her sons in the Kensington area, which she knew well and liked, and she asked the estate agents Knight Frank & Rutley to give her details of suitable residences. However, she soon discovered that it was not as easy as it seemed. As she was mother to the heir and the spare, security considerations were uppermost. In her opinion, few houses, if any, were suitable. By the beginning of 1994, she had decided that she had to stay at Kensington Palace for her boys' safety. She was agitated about possible attacks, not only from terrorists, but from the media. The costs involved in securing an alternative London home, when she examined them, seemed to be prohibitive. As a further justification for staying, the princess told friends: 'Why should I make it easy for my husband?' arguing if she left Kensington Palace she would simply be playing into his hands by making it easier for him to finesse her away from the royal family and any future influence over her children. Possession, to her mind, was nine-tenths of the law.

Yet her continued tenure at Kensington Palace symbolizes her ambiguous status and her ambivalent approach to her future. Her London home is a place of bitter memories, dashed hopes, angry confrontations and restrictions on her movements. While no longer the scene of raging arguments, the shadow of Prince Charles still looms large. Essentially, her paralysis of inaction lies within. Since her separation and more recently her withdrawal from royal duties, there is no real reason why she should not move, though the bomb at the Israeli Embassy in Kensington in July 1994 is a reminder that security is always going to be a problem.

These days it is appropriate to describe the princess as a prisoner of her own making, a captive of her psyche. Diana's semi-private position suggests that she is now free to follow her own star. She has won a measure of freedom but not full emancipation. The door of the gilded cage is open. Now she must find the will to fly away.

4

'It's Time to Grow Up'

FINALLY, IT ALL BECAME TOO MUCH FOR HER. She sat at her paper-strewn desk, her head held in her hands, salty tears rolling down her pink cheeks. The paparazzi were making her life a misery. They followed her from the minute she stepped out of her West Kensington home to the moment she returned. While she accepted the need for an armed police bodyguard he did rather put a wet blanket on her royal romance. She couldn't even hold her prince's hand in the car; he drove the car while the royal protection officer sat in the passenger seat. 'I know exactly what Princess Diana went through and is going through. Exactly,' said Sophie Rhys-Jones, the young woman expected to marry Prince Edward.

Of course the Queen had been sweet, far friendlier than Sophie could ever have imagined. The rest of the royal family were charming, although she often had to stifle a smile in their company, as their mannerisms were just too like the television puppet satire, *Spitting Image*. Yet she knew instinctively that she couldn't unburden her worries and concerns on to any of them: the Queen, her family or the courtiers. It was the same with the prince she loved. Naturally he would be sympathetic, but he would never truly be able to understand. 'Never complain, never explain' was the Windsor's unofficial motto. When she joined in their games and talk at Sandringham and Balmoral the chatter was light, bright and ultimately trite. She realized that there would always be a gulf between royalty and commoner.

Yet the problems of the ambitious public relations executive who wooed a minor prince were but a trifle compared with the continuing tribulations endured by the Princess of Wales. For a start Edward and Sophie were still in the first throes of romance, the media interest modest and the potential burden of royal responsibilities moderate. None the less, for Sophie, a well-travelled, relatively sophisticated girl of the world, the culture of majesty had quickly turned from a rosy dream to a nightmare of vexation and frustration. 'If it wasn't for the royal business, Edward and I would be sublimely happy,' she is fond of telling friends.

For the Princess of Wales 'the royal business' had

virtually destroyed her life, physically and emotionally. During the winter of 1992, she warily took her first steps as a semi-detached princess. Increasingly, Diana was becoming irritated by the police presence, intensely aware that the media were seeking any candidate for the billing: 'Di's new love', and she was constantly looking over her shoulder, fearful that Prince Charles and his allies were plotting against her. The competition between Charles and Diana which was such a feature of their last months together was continuing, much to the chagrin of courtiers. Conspiracies, real or imagined, clouded Diana's thinking. At the same time, well-meaning friends, advisers and courtiers bombarded her with so much conflicting advice that her head was spinning. Friends or foes, everyone wanted the princess dangling from their string.

Just as the men in grey suits at Buckingham Palace were reflecting on a disastrous 1992, the Princess of Wales was also starting 1993 at a low ebb. A holiday with her boys on the island of Nevis in the Caribbean helped recharge the batteries. The Montpelier Plantation Inn, where Diana stayed, is a select but not 'luxurious' hotel, owned by old Etonian, James Milnes-Gaskell and his wife Celia. When gathered for dinner on the verandah overlooking the sea, the princess's fellow guests remarked on how friendly and approachable she was. However, it was a long while before she fired on all cylinders. At photo calls under the tropical sun she put a brave face on her troubles, but privately she was a woman lamenting her lost innocence, a failed relationship and the wasted years of her adult life. Her mood was reflected in her frequent choice of black clothes—she bridled when she was described by one woman journalist as 'dowdy'. 'She was in mourning,' reflects a friend, 'but she is also saying that she no longer wishes to be judged at all by her fashions. There was this maturing sense of her own worth, not wanting to be seen as simply a clotheshorse.' At moments of optimism Diana felt she could beat the royal system and use her position in a more positive way. Often, though, the aspiring New Model princess was so absorbed in her own troubles that her depression sometimes led to her becoming self-obsessed and oblivious to the needs of her friends and supporters. Understandably, during those first months, she felt unsure of her future, alienated from her husband, alone in a hostile system, and at the mercy of the media. Diana placed great store by the forecast of her astrologer, who had predicted that 1993 was going to be *annus horribilis* II.

Yet the wrath of the gods—or rather the tabloid media—fell on the head of Prince Charles first of all. A tape-recorded conversation, intimate and distasteful, allegedly between Charles and Camilla Parker Bowles, was published in tabloid newspapers. For several months the threat to publish and damn the royal intimates had hung over Charles. When the thread finally snapped it forced many in the Crown's traditional constituency—the Church, the military and Parliament—to question his fitness to rule and others to wonder if there was a plot inside the British security forces to discredit the royal family.

Neither Charles nor Camilla has ever denied that the taped conversation was genuine. Diana certainly had no doubts since the sentiments expressed fully justified her suspicions about the nature of their relationship. Totally convinced that the tape was a conversation between her husband and Camilla, Diana was still shocked to read the sordid details in cold print. During the lewd, late-night telephone chat, which had allegedly taken place on 18 December 1989 while Charles was staying at the Cheshire home of his old friend, Anne, Duchess of Westminster, there is little doubt about the couple's undying affection for one another. After various words of endearment from the woman, the man tells her: 'Your great achievement is to love me,' adding, 'You suffer all these indignities and tortures and calumnies.' The woman responds with: 'I'd suffer anything for you. That's love. It's the strength of love.' The 1,574-word transcript included a coarse joke about the man being turned into a Tampax tampon so that he could be constantly joined with the wife of one of his oldest friends. Just before he rings off the man says he will 'press the tit', that is, the phone button. The woman replies: 'I wish you were pressing mine.' The man replies: 'I love you, I adore you,' and the woman says: 'I do love you.'

Appalled and sickened, Diana read the transcript with mounting anger as she noted the names of so many friends, people she had known for years and trusted, who had conspired with the prince and Camilla to deceive her by providing cover stories or safe houses where they could meet in secret. It revived memories of her courtship when his circle deftly used to change the subject at the mention of Camilla, of the flowers Charles used to send her using their pet names, Fred and Gladys, the bracelet he gave Camilla on the eve of his wedding inscribed with those same initials, and the photographs of Camilla that had fluttered out of his diary during their ill-fated honeymoon. Diana told friends that she had discussed her husband's relationship with Camilla with the Queen on numerous occasions, their first conversation taking place only a few years after the marriage. The princess knew early on that the royal family were well-aware of the prince's confidante. In fact, during one acrimonious conversation with her husband, Prince Charles left her in no doubt that as far as Prince Philip was concerned, Charles could return to his 'Highgrove friends' if their marriage failed. Diana did not need a map to work out to whom her father-in-law was referring.

While Diana nursed her anger and sense of betrayal, Charles felt the crown slipping from his grasp as leading churchmen and other Establishment figures registered their obvious disquiet. One cabinet minister remarked: 'He would be well-advised to break all connections with Mrs Parker Bowles and start off with a clean slate.' There was also debate about whether the coronation oath should be altered, as well as the Church's relationship with the State and hence the royal family. The Archdeacon of York declared: 'The Queen could die tomorrow and it would raise all sorts of problems. It would make things very difficult if Charles were to divorce and remarry.' Other churchmen felt that his behaviour 'disqualified' him from office, while senior Army officers privately expressed doubts about his position of colonel-in-chief of six regiments. The scandal did evoke moments of black humour. By chance a group of Americans were visiting Highgrove at the time the story broke. One woman guest told the prince: 'By the way, sir, I do approve of your choice in older women.' The prince, nonplussed by the boldness of this comment, replied: 'It would take an American to say that.'

It was not only Charles who faced the wrath of the media, however. A leaked letter from Lord McGregor, the chairman of the Press Complaints Commission, to Sir David Calcutt, who was at the time preparing an official report on invasion of privacy by newspapers, firmly blamed the princess for manipulating the media in the months leading up to the royal separation. He singled out Diana for blame in spite of the fact that two tabloid newspapers publicly stated that they had been used by Charles's friends to state his case. 'I am satisfied that the intrusions into the private lives of the Prince and Princess of Wales were intrusions contrived by the princess herself and her entourage,' he said. The episode, which lead to lurid headlines like 'Diana in the Dock' provoked strong condemnation from Members of Parliament and other Establishment figures. 'If she is not careful, I fear she will find herself greatly reduced,' commented the Bishop of Peterborough, adding: 'If you live by the media you should die by the media.'

It was galling for Diana, especially as she had been tried and convicted on statements based on hearsay evidence. During her childhood and adult life she has always endeavoured to be seen in the best possible light, often to the annoyance of her family and friends, obsessed with avoiding blame, for whatever misdemeanour. She felt her husband's exposure had been dealt with leniently with the blame being deflected on to her. She was so distracted by the furore that, when she took the boys to their Berkshire school, her Ford car was involved in a minor collision with her police back-up vehicle. For a woman who prides herself on her ability behind the wheel it was a sure sign of her inner turmoil.

Suspicion shadowed every dealing between the princess and the Palace, fired by a media and her own paranoia, determined to read conspiracy into every script. Yet, while no Palace plots materialized, there was obvious hostility towards Diana inside the Palace and among the wider aristocracy. 'I can't find anybody inside the Palace with a good word to say for her,' said one visitor. Although officials themselves insisted: 'The aim is not to isolate Diana, far from it.'

At Buckingham Palace the strategy is, and always has been, to support the sovereign and sustain the monarchy, and Diana has always adhered to this, once commenting: 'The monarchy has existed for a thousand years. Who am I to come along and change it just like that.' As far as the Palace is concerned the needs of the sovereign and her immediate heirs are paramount; as a mere 'in-law', the princess is by definition an also-ran. But the Palace was unclear about Diana's future plans, aware of her disenchantment with the way the Windsor show was managed, and becoming increasingly disturbed by her relations with the media. Uncertainty at the top quickly filtered down to the roots of the Establishment. A number of Lords Lieutenant, plumed worthies who organize royal visits in their counties, wondered aloud if the princess should still be treated as a full-blown royal: small details of protocol, like the number and status of the dignitaries sent to greet the princess on official visits, were debated at length.

Whatever the personal feelings of the Queen's men towards Diana, their primary purpose was to serve the sovereign, her son and the status quo. To this end they attempted the almost impossible task of resurrecting Prince Charles's public image at the price of reducing the status of the Princess of Wales, whom they readily acknowledged was still the shining star in a fading royal firmament. If their vision for the Prince of Wales cut across the undefined ambitions of the Princess of Wales, then so be it.

However she played her hand, Diana found that her estranged husband held the aces. When she expressed a wish to visit the troops and refugees in Bosnia under the auspices of the Red Cross, she was told that Prince Charles's plans would take precedence. As a result it was the prince, in his capacity of colonel-in-chief, who flew out to see the Cheshire regiment who formed part of the United Nations peace-keeping force. In September 1993, Diana was thwarted again by the Palace when she arranged a private visit to see the Irish President, Mary Robinson, in Dublin. Officially she was told that she could not meet the woman she greatly respected for 'security reasons', even though two months later she attended the Remembrance Service in Enniskillen, Northern Ireland. Privately she suspected that the Establishment did not want her to enjoy such a high political profile and inevitably overshadow her estranged husband. Her suspicions were confirmed when Prince Charles met the Irish president at the launch of the Warrington Memorial Fund, set up following the deaths of two young boys killed by the IRA.

During the winter of 1993 when she made secret plans to see the American business motivator, Anthony Robbins, in Washington, the Foreign Office tied themselves in knots trying to prevent the meeting. Initially they said that they had security information about a dangerous loner with a fixation about the royal family. Then, when she dismissed their fears as absurd, they told her that, as so many high-ranking royals were out of the country, either on holiday or public duties, she had to stay in Britain to 'mind the store'. Little wonder then that when she watched Nigel Short play Boris Kasparov in the world chess championship she saw in the game a metaphor of her own position. 'It's my life,' she said, 'I'm just a pawn pushed around by the powers that be.'

Her feelings were echoed by the Duchess of York, who in July 1993 felt the full weight of the Palace and Foreign Office bear down on her when she was offered and accepted the position of Goodwill Ambassador for the Geneva-based United Nations High Commission for Refugees, the organization responsible for the welfare of the world's 39 million displaced people. Her decision rattled the Establishment, who let it be known that they considered the duchess, with her party-going profile, 'entirely unsuitable' for the post. 'They are out to get me,' the duchess confided to friends at the height of the controversy. Her friend Pida Ripley, the founder of the women's refugee charity Women Aid, who initially sponsored the duchess, was more forthright. 'This is quite simply a witch-hunt against the duchess and somebody has got to say it is time to call it off.'

While in general her relations with Buckingham Palace were fragile and framed with suspicion, the Princess of Wales was grateful for press office assistance from time to time. The Queen's press secretary used the weight of his office to defuse a potentially damaging story when a prominent Catholic priest, Father Anthony Sutch, claimed that Diana was seriously considering Catholicism. After intervention from the Palace, Father Sutch issued a statement saying that he either 'exaggerated or lied'. A year later, when Diana's mother quietly converted to Catholicism, the princess was again grateful for Palace assistance in dealing with the media.

Her appreciation of assistance on such occasions was more than matched by her exasperation with a system which subtly straitjacketed or sidelined her ambitions and proposals. Her frustration came to a head in autumn 1993 following a series of sympathetic newspaper articles about the changing face of the monarchy, which were based on briefings by Sir Robert Fellowes and other officials. In one comment, an unnamed courtier patronizingly commented: 'Diana is headstrong but we must show her love and understanding and bend over backwards to avoid a chasm in the early stages because, if she became bitter and twisted, it would be impossible for the children.' Furious at this portrayal of her as a foolish child, she spoke angrily to Sir Robert Fellowes. She told him that not only was she sick of being used as newspaper fodder but that this kind of story merely threw petrol on the flames of speculation about her life.

Jousting with the Palace juggernaut was one thing; full-scale battle with Prince Charles in his St James's Palace redoubt was quite another. As far as the prince and his camp were concerned, Diana was public-enemy number one. The sense of betrayal and bad blood could not, would not, be expunged. As courtiers have found down the ages, the difficulty in working for the royal family is the uneasy amalgam of public duties and private life. As the estranged Prince and Princess of Wales were jockeying for public popularity while dickering over their divorce, royal officials inevitably were caught in the crossfire.

One of the first victims of this internecine warfare was their press officer, Dickie Arbiter. For many months Prince Charles believed that the former radio reporter was playing double agent: feeding information about his diary dates and other plans to Diana so that she could work out a counter-strategy to steal the limelight. Charles frequently complained: 'I'm highly suspicious of him, he works for my wife.' As a result the prince recruited several friends to feed false stories into the system believing that they would filter through to the princess via Arbiter. In this way he hoped to lead his wife a merry dance, expose the suspected culprit or culprits and, with any luck, embarrass the princess into the bargain.

Yet at the same time Diana suspected that the hapless Arbiter was informing the prince about her own schemes, while deliberately playing down her public duties in order to highlight the prince. On one occasion she tore to shreds a handwritten note from Arbiter, who had tried to explain why she had only enjoyed modest media coverage for a speech on behalf of the Red Cross. Eventually Arbiter was kept so much in the dark by both warring parties that he had to ring sympathetic journalists to find out what was going on. He now works in the calmer waters of the Royal Collections.

Their mutual suspicion reached such a fever pitch that Prince Charles advised his friends to have their homes swept for bugging devices in case her side were listening in to their telephone conversations. Indeed, if Charles happened to see Diana on the telephone in her office at St James's Palace he felt physically sick. 'That woman is possessed by the telephone,' he told friends, convinced that she was passing on all the Palace secrets to her pals.

Paranoia continued at the Palace and, since the various illicit taping scandals, all the royal residences, including Balmoral and Sandringham, are regularly swept for listening devices. Even the royal toilets get the full treatment. This sensitive work is undertaken by the police, as private companies are not given high enough security clearance. For Diana, one question remained unanswered: who guards the guards? She wanted to be sure that the police who swept her apartment were not acting on behalf of the royal Establishment or her husband.

Her fears did have some substance. For many months accusing fingers had been pointed at MI5, the Government security service, for its suspected involvement in releasing the Squidgy, Camilla and Fergie tapes. It was a view that resurfaced with the publication of a fourth tape, this time of an alleged conversation between Charles and Diana at Highgrove the previous November. While this one was quickly revealed as an elaborate hoax—neither party had met at Highgrove during that month, and, in fact, the first week of November, they spent in Korea on an official visit—there were still many unanswered questions about the original tapes. Cyril

Reenan, the retired bank manager who recorded the Squidgy tape, further muddied the waters by claiming that he had first heard it four days after the conversation between the princess and her male admirer actually took place. It meant that the royal conversation had been recorded and then re-broadcast by some shadowy agency in the hope that a radio ham would finally pick it up. All very peculiar, especially as the head of MI5, Stella Rimington, categorically denied any security service involvement. Other odd occurrences were to follow.

The Duchess of York had secretly visited a lawyer, based in central London, to discuss the legal details of her divorce. A few days later, the lawyer's office was burgled and all files and computer discs relating to their discussion were stolen. No other office in the chambers where the lawyer worked with many colleagues was tampered with. A few weeks after this incident in May 1993, Diana's close-protection officers checked out the LA Fitness Centre in west London, where it was rumoured Diana had been secretly photographed. While their investigations proved inconclusive, the princess's personal trainer, Carol Ann Brown, soon left the gym, and Diana, her suspicions raised, transferred to a rival fitness centre. Six months later, amid intense controversy, the gym owner, Bryce Taylor, sold photographs of Diana working out for a six-figure sum. At the same time as the police examination of Diana's gym, several friends told of their own close encounters of a troubling kind.

A worried Captain James Hewitt asked for her

advice on how to handle being followed every time he ventured forth from his Devon home. Hewitt, who was enjoying a secret friendship with TV weather girl Sally Faber, the wife of a West Country Member of Parliament, was unclear whether his shadows were journalists, private detectives or Special Branch policemen. Another of Diana's male friends had a brush with the state security service, MI5, in a most roundabout manner. Out of curiosity, he asked a police friend to run a computer check on his own phone. Within two hours an MI5 operative had contacted the police officer to ask why he was interested in that particular phone line. The clear implication was that MI5 was already monitoring the telephone of Diana's friend. Occasionally the princess and the duchess saw the funny side of their predicament. During one telephone conversation they were discussing the Queen Mother, whom they both distrust. When they finished speaking their minds about her, Fergie joked: 'If MI5 are listening the Queen Mother is a great lady and we hope she lives for ever.'

These were curious coincidences, and the princess decided not to take any chances. Secretly, she hired a private agency to sweep her telephones for listening devices. When her butler Harold Brown raised an eyebrow she explained that they were there to clean the carpet. The operation would have passed unnoticed if the security experts had not visited the police lodge, which houses a bank of security cameras, and asked to check the phone lines. There was immediate consternation among the constables and irritation from the police inspectors who felt humiliated by the princess's action. Diana faced an interview with angry senior Metropolitan Police officers with equanimity. 'I don't trust anybody here,' she told her interlocutors. 'It's my home and I shall do what I want in it.' While no listening devices were found, it is a measure of the atmosphere inside the Palace that the princess felt such action necessary. As a final act in this farce, the police re-swept her apartment to make sure the private firm had not bugged her.

If her home life was becoming increasingly intolerable, her office milieu was virtually impossible, with 'his' and 'her' staff working cheek by jowl in the confined conditions of St James's Palace. For a time after the separation, Diana considered transferring her modest staff, who she called the 'A-team', from St James's to Kensington Palace. Eventually she decided against the idea, worried that she would find it more difficult to find out what the other side were plotting. Isolated, depressed and nervy, the princess spent much time, her friends thought far too much, fretting about Charles's plans. On one occasion in February 1993, she spent a day on tenterhooks when the prince's private secretary, Richard Aylard, unexpectedly requested a meeting with her chief aide, Patrick Jephson. She instantly jumped to the conclusion that the prince was going to outline terms for a divorce settlement. In the end her fears were groundless. It was simply a routine administrative meeting.

Other misgivings did have substance. Shortly before she flew to Nepal in March 1993 on her first overseas visit since the separation, Charles's courtiers hosted a reception for media folk, where it was made clear that her trip was not expected to be a success. This message was reinforced on the tour itself when several journalists told her privately that Charles's camp was keen to see her fall on her face. Again, an embarrassing leak announcing that the princess had been considered and then rejected as a candidate for the prestigious Dimbleby lecture had the fingerprints of Charles's supporters all over it.

During 1993 the battle of the Waleses was fought out as much in the media as behind the scenes, as each attempted to win the hearts and minds of the public. Early in the New Year, Charles's visit to Mexico and America, undertaken with much apprehension in the light of the Camillagate tape, was considered a resounding success. The very public announcement of his decision to give up serious polo so that he could spend more time with his children and chair a new committee on the Royal Collections, which would tie in neatly with both his domestic and public concerns, was widely welcomed. By the summer there were nine officials working directly or indirectly on his portfolio of well-publicized interests or improving his image. The salary bill alone was around £300,000, while the princess, whose staff were paid from the prince's estate of the Duchy of Cornwall, made do with a part-time press officer.

For a princess used to an adoring media, this change in fortunes undermined her precarious self-esteem and fed her existing anxieties. While she saw her husband bask in the glow of media approval, she found herself accused of being a media junkie, lurching from one photo call to another: a holiday in the Caribbean, riding a log flume at Thorpe Park leisure park and skiing with her children. Lord Wyatt, a friend of the Queen Mother, wrote: 'Princess Diana could never have won a university place but she won a prince and failed to keep him. She is addicted to the limelight her marriage brought. It's like a drug. To feed her craving she will do anything, even if it means destroying the throne she solemnly swore to uphold.'

The occasion of the funeral of Diana's grandmother, Ruth, Lady Fermoy, in July 1993 symbolized the silliness and sadness of this rather pathetic media one-upmanship. On the night before the funeral, which took place in Norfolk, Prince Charles and the Queen Mother stayed at Wood Farm on the Sandringham estate. Diana flew up by helicopter. There were two cars waiting, one containing the Queen Mother and Prince Charles, the other for Diana. Immediately realizing that this could be construed as a very public demonstration of her isolation from the royal family, the princess insisted on accompanying her husband, showing the world that, while they were separated, they could at least behave in a civilized manner. Charles initially demurred but, not wanting a public scene, quickly agreed.

Like two gladiators circling round one another, the incident illustrates how both the Prince and Princess of Wales constantly kept up their guard. However, on the way to St Margaret's Church in King's Lynn, the princess felt tired and ill, having just returned from a four-day visit to Zimbabwe. After the funeral, she had two official engagements to attend: a garden party at Buckingham Palace and then the premiere of the Steven Spielberg film, Jurassic Park. She really didn't think she was well enough to go to both and, in a rare display of frankness, broached the subject with Charles and asked what he thought she should do. His advice was to give up the garden party, rest in the afternoon and then appear at the film premiere. She felt torn by competing impulses, on the one hand wanting to believe that he spoke out of concern for her health, yet worried that he was pursuing an ulterior motive. As the garden party is a time-honoured if tedious royal function—'zoo teas' the Queen Mother dismissively calls them—she wondered if he was deliberately steering her in the direction of the showbiz event so that she could be criticized for forsaking the public for Hollywood stars. In this trying time the princess, vulnerable, isolated and unwell, wanted a consoling shoulder to lean on, and above all a companion. Maybe deep down she wanted love, not war. In the end she could not trust herself to believe that his motives were true and she attended both functions.

Ironically, this revealing episode occurred when a cabal of unofficial, middle-aged male advisers, including millionaire businessman Lord Palumbo and Sir Gordon Reece, were working behind the scenes to effect a reconciliation between the warring Waleses. Under the plan, codenamed 'Flavia', after the tragic princess in *The Prisoner of Zenda* who was loved by everyone except her husband, the royal couple would gradually spend more time together in public and private. The aim was to show that, while the couple lived apart, they were working together on behalf of the monarchy and country. It was a romantic dream, which probably says more about the quixotic delusions of these white knights who fancied themselves as queenmakers rather than the true feelings of the royal couple.

In reality, as the months passed, competition between the Prince and Princess of Wales seemed to intensify rather than diminish. As ever, their children were at the centre of the most ferocious battles. Tart memos about who would have William and Harry over Christmas 1993, and for how long, were exchanged as early as June. It was finally agreed that the boys would be based at Sandringham, the Queen's Norfolk retreat, although each parent would enjoy their children's company for half the school holidays. Unknown to Prince Charles, the Queen had invited Diana to spend Christmas Eve with the royal family so that she could join the boys in opening their presents—a custom dating back to Queen Alexandra —and the following morning attend the church service before leaving for Kensington Palace. Prince Charles did not discover this until November when a member of his staff, rather than the Queen, informed him. He phoned Diana and asked peevishly if she had discussed it with their children. Emphasizing that she was only staying for a day, Diana informed him that not only the Queen but also William and Harry had asked her to come. As far as she was concerned his reaction merely underlined his increasing remoteness from the rest of his family, and his suspicion, bordering on the paranoiac, of her every move and gesture. On one occasion, quite by chance, the Duchess of York spotted Prince Charles and his sons driving along the M4 motorway to spend the weekend at Highgrove. She subsequently phoned Diana and mentioned this accidental sighting. When the princess asked Charles how the boys had enjoyed their weekend he was instantly guarded, demanding to know how she had found out where they were.

Public evidence of the yawning gulf between Charles and Diana was provided by the squabble over which Christmas card each would send, a year after the separation. Both realized that the family group on the front of these cards would be pored over by royal Kremlinologists in the media. Diana suggested that, for appearance's sake, they send separate cards but with the same picture of their boys. This at least would send the signal that even though the prince and princess were separated, the boys still came first. The idea was a nonstarter. 'Charles wouldn't dream of it,' remarked the princess. Indeed, when it was raised with Prince Charles, he was surprised that she was sending her own Christmas cards at all. So the princess organized a session with society photographer, Earl Drogheda, during the boys' school half-term. Charles decided instead to issue a photograph of himself with his sons at Balmoral, taken during the filming of Jonathan Dimbleby's documentary. As Diana predicted, the media feasted on the sad tidings of an unhappy family torn apart.

The Queen's men were alarmed at the competition in their relationship and the effect it was having on the children. They wondered for instance if it was appropriate for William and Harry to be enjoying so many glamorous holidays during their school breaks. One week Charles took them on a luxury cruise aboard a billionaire's yacht, the next Diana whisked them to Disney World in Florida. When Prince Charles went to Balmoral during Easter in 1994, he took a vanload of entertainments for the two princes, including a set of soccer goal posts, a badminton set, two mountain bikes, a trampoline, guns, and small trailbikes worth £2000 each. Who benefited, the boys or their parents? Lord Tebbit's aide Beryl Goldsmith made public those doubts saying: 'The princes are the most pampered children in the land, showered with far too many material goodies.' Child-psychology expert Susan Jenner conceded: 'If all these wonderful trips are setting them apart from their school friends, their development could very well be hindered.'

Faced with, at best, indifference from Buckingham Palace and open disdain from her husband's retinue, it is not surprising that Diana felt herself under siege throughout 1993. Unlike Prince Charles, Diana has no pre-ordained career. For the first time in her life she was flying solo and was aware that it would be a bumpy ride. 'I will make mistakes,' she told confidantes valiantly, 'but that will not stop me from doing

what I feel is right.' Her constitutional po
simply that of the mother to the future king.
the machinations of the Palace, nobody co
that away from her. But her public role was becoming
increasingly unclear. Although still the most popular
member of the royal family, she was now at arm's
length from the monarchy and embarking on the
difficult task of redefining her royal role.

The theme of her first year on the fringe of the
family was her attempted transition from a life where
she saw herself as a puppet of the system to a more
fulfilling existence where she was in command of her
destiny. It was not an easy change, psychologically or
politically. She was once asked what was the worst
moment of her life and she replied: 'Oh, that's easy,
the day I walked down the aisle at St Paul's Cathedral.
I felt that my personality was taken away from me and
I was taken over by the royal machine.'

The implications of marrying so young into the
royal family were that during her formative twenties,
when most young adults strike out on their own, the
princess gradually succumbed to the rigid embrace of
the institution of monarchy. She was unused to
exercising free will or expressing her choices except
within narrow confines made by others. Her belief, at
times all consuming, in the predictions of her astrologer, shows how little value she placed on her own
instincts and judgment. The astrologer had forecast
for example that the end of 1993 would bring a
'golden opportunity' for the princess in the form of a
prestigious job, and while Diana waited for this

chance to drop into her lap, the more sceptical of her friends suggested that people make their own luck in life. Diana's insecurity and self-denigration were compounded by those in her circle who exploited her low self-esteem. The princess told one visitor to Kensington Palace that from the moment she woke up in the morning she had managed to run herself down so far that by lunchtime she felt that her life had less value than 'a cockroach living in Bulgaria'. Her maturity was in recognizing that for a decade she had been anaesthetized from reality; her challenge was bravely to embrace her new world.

Yet the princess is no royal rebel, far from it. She has learned enough during her decade inside the Firm to toe the party line. As she once remarked to a friend: 'When I go to the Palace for a garden party or a summit meeting I am a very different person. I conform to what is expected of me so that they can't find fault when I am in their presence.' If she had a free hand she would only tinker at the edges of the monarchy; she finds the Queen's Christmas broadcast 'cringe-making' because it is so stilted; she would cut down on the glamorous occasions and introduce garden parties at Buckingham Palace specially for the handicapped and wheelchair-bound. Essentially, her discontent lies in the manner and style of the British monarchy, the brittle formality and mind-numbing irrelevance of so much of royal life. Royals down the decades have made similar, often half-hearted, complaints, but the princess felt instinctively that if she could change the style of her public life she could enhance the substance of her contribution to the nation. 'I want to help the man in the street,' she once said. In her heart she is a woman who is happier with the people rather than her people.

A more relaxed style, spontaneity blending with informality, was her general ambition. She admires the modesty of the Scandinavian monarchies and the resolute independence of Princess Anne, whose work for The Save the Children Fund has earned her international respect. Diana wanted that—and more. With no precedents in the diplomats' royal etiquette book on how to treat a separated Princess of Wales, Diana now had an opportunity to make her own rules and set her own pace. 'This needs a woman's touch' was her refrain, a sentiment that revealed a developing feminism in her private and public life. Her undoubted cynicism towards the opposite sex following the failure of her marriage was reinforced by long conversations with divorced girlfriends like Catherine Soames and her growing friendship with Sandra Horley, chief executive of Refuge, a shelter for battered women in Chiswick, west London. She admires women like former Prime Minister Margaret Thatcher, Irish President Mary Robinson, and Minister for Overseas Development Lynda Chalker because they have displayed the ability and willpower to succeed in a man's world. Indeed, such is her fascination with Lady Thatcher, that she spent much time in the autumn of 1993 trying to arrange a private dinner with her. Unfortunately, she was busy promoting her memoirs at the time. A friend recalls: 'After her first

Christmas alone she was very much feeling her way as an individual. There was a necessary introspection and grieving as she reviewed her relationship with Prince Charles.'

At the same time, Diana profoundly understood the value of her position as Princess of Wales. She knew that her standing in society, both at home and abroad, gave her a unique springboard from which to support the causes and issues she cherished. The revelation that Diana had suffered from bulimia nervosa had touched many women around the world, prompting thousands of sufferers to seek help and the setting up of specialist clinics to deal with the problem. Housewife Patsy Richards, whose marriage broke down after ten years, commented: 'My marriage didn't end because of Princess Diana, but she's certainly been a great role model, and given me inspiration, watching her going through what I am and coming out the other end has been a big help.' While the princess was embarrassed and rather touched by the public response to her own problems, she had begun to realize the international dimension of her appeal. Her work for AIDS—itself a sign of her boldness in choosing a challenging rather than traditional issue—showed how she could cut across national boundaries. Overseas work was stimulating, not only because it gave her a different stage to that occupied by her husband, but also because it was away from the gimlet eye of Buckingham Palace.

Her trip to Nepal in March 1993 reflected many of the threads of her public life. The media, now defining Diana in terms of her separation, dwelt on the signs that her five-day visit was to be her one-way ticket to second-class status. Serenaded with 'Colonel Bogey' rather than the national anthem on her arrival, she stayed in the British Embassy rather than the royal palace, while the King of Nepal merely met her for dinner instead of playing official host. 'We may be witnessing early signs that Diana is no longer a royal of the first order,' announced one portentous headline.

It was not as simple as that. While the text of 'Princess versus Palace' was transparent, there were other sub-plots. The newspapers and columnists, who had nailed their colours to her husband's mast, were spoiling for conflict. Invariably the columnists were elderly or middle-aged men whose opinions veered towards misogyny. Diana knew that the conservative *Telegraph* group was behind Prince Charles, and so was unsurprised when it was their correspondent who first pointed out her 'second-class status'. She smiled knowingly when she noted how the Palace themselves admonished the *Daily Telegraph* for their overly flattering coverage of the prince's visit to the Arabian Gulf later that year. There were other media sharks sensing royal blood. Sunday newspaper columnists like John Junor and octogenarian peer Woodrow Wyatt were persistently hostile. On several occasions Diana used the one weapon at her disposal —her charm—to disarm her critics. By chance she encountered Junor on Kensington High Street. She deliberately set out to flatter the dour Scotsman, and was delighted to see the dramatic change in his comments about her which followed. Again she was at her most enchanting one evening at the Dorchester when she encountered Lord Fawsley, an influential constitutional expert and friend of Prince Charles's. Afterwards he was most complimentary, saying that he had 'misjudged' her and offered to assist her if possible. Men of a certain age have always been easy prey for the princess.

While the media watched for conspiracies, they lost the plot themselves, failing to see that the low-key, informal Nepalese visit was requested by the princess herself. She had recognized the public's desire for a more modest and relevant monarchy, a wish that neatly coincided with her objectives of reshaping her public royal life in her own image. Her skill in public life has been the intuitive ability to use her office to promote her causes while her compassionate nature draws her to the dying, diseased and dispossessed. It is a potent combination. 'I will never complain again,' she said as she emerged from a one-room airless hut in one mountain village, a comment which both expressed her own sympathies while making headlines worldwide. The inclusion of her sister Sarah as lady-in-waiting, her decision to fly by scheduled airline and her desire to dispense with protocol and get down to business symbolized the style of this unassuming Princess of Wales. Unlike her husband, she even charmed the 'ratpack'—the band of royal reporters who follow the Windsor wagon train around the world. On the flight home she sent a bottle of champagne to the *Daily Mail*'s Richard Kay, a reporter who would prove a useful conduit over the coming months.

She was learning to build up an alternative court, an array of influential supporters who would help her circumvent the enemy, as she saw it, at Buckingham Palace. During the visit the princess made a firm friend and political ally of the Minister for Overseas Development, Lynda Chalker. The feeling was entirely mutual. 'I look on her as my favourite niece,' says Baroness Chalker, while for the next few months the princess peppered her conversations with 'Lynda says this' and 'Lynda says that'. When the princess was organizing another visit to Zimbabwe and felt that the Foreign Office were dragging their feet, she went straight to the top, speaking directly to the Foreign Secretary, Douglas Hurd, and Lynda Chalker. This is one of the many contradictions about her public persona. While Diana fights shy of the 'men in grey' she has absolutely no compunction about going to the boss of any organization and arguing her case. Wary of Palace courtiers, she makes a point of phoning the Queen—'the chief lady'—at least once a week. 'She admires her stoicism,' says a friend. She has also ensured that the boys, William and Harry, frequently see their grandmother to underscore the fact that she is the 'king mother'. It tickles the princess to see how easily charmed the Queen is by her grandsons. Mischievous Prince Harry became one of the few men in her life ever to compliment the Queen on her fashions. His remark, 'That's a pretty dress', during tea one afternoon brought a girlish blush to Her Majesty's cheeks.

As part of her 'charm offensive' she has wined and dined newspaper editors and publishers, television pundits and other movers and shakers in the world of ballet, the arts and society. She woos from a certain New-Age perspective, assessing the personalities of the powerful by their astrological star signs. When, for example, it seemed that Prime Minister John Major was about to be supplanted by the Chancellor of the Exchequer, Kenneth Clarke, she checked Clarke's star sign to capture a flavour of his personality. As a Piscean, he has characteristics of wisdom and intuition, but is prone to aimlessness. According to the Prime Minister's Aries star sign, he can be headstrong, impulsive, self-righteous and naive. The princess often explains the actions of her friends by reference to characteristics typical of their particular signs of the zodiac. This application of astrology to her personal life is a weapon in her armoury as she attempts to take control of her life, a determination fuelled by her distrust of the Palace and her resolution no longer to be a puppet of the system.

Outsiders detected a fresh mood in their dealings with her office. 'Oh, I'll go and ask her about it,' her press officer Geoff Crawford said to one newspaper executive in response to a question about her activities. 'That would never have happened in the past,' he observed. For a time she enjoyed favourable coverage in the *Daily Mail* thanks to judicious leaks through her circle. As the subtle competition between the prince and princess intensified, Diana utilized the public relations skills of Sir Gordon Reece, the former press secretary to Margaret Thatcher, to place favourable stories. She is sensitive to newspaper criticism and yet, in spite of endless pleadings from her friends, she continues to lap up every word they write about her. Once again it is an example of her achingly low self-esteem, happy only when she is being praised by others, desolate when blamed. As a close friend put it, 'Her deepest fear is being forgotten or neglected.'

Her attempts to cut the strings of control had numerous satisfying by-products. Diana insisted on opening all her mail herself, a morning routine, which she felt brought her in closer contact with her public. The letters, usually diffident in style, contained homilies, felicitations and accounts of difficult personal experiences. The princess was deeply touched by many of them. 'Your motives are of the highest, great things are in store for you. Trust your instincts and intuitions,' were the sentiments in one heartfelt letter. A Canadian couple whose friend had AIDS wrote to thank her for her courageous work on behalf of sufferers worldwide. They explained that they had initially rejected their friend, but that her example had given them the fortitude to face him. In gratitude, they wrote to Diana at Kensington Palace: 'We all need and require, from time to time, a little praise for what we do or say that touches a person's life.'

The royal life that had once constrained her impulses, she now endeavoured to mould to suit her ambitions. During her married years she had spoken wistfully of visiting Paris. With a trio of girlfriends, she now travelled there by private jet, the enjoyment of which was only partly spoiled by preying paparazzi. A week-long excursion in July to the holiday villa of her friend, Catherine Soames, in the South of France remained secret. She decided to see for herself the world chess championship between the losing Briton, Nigel Short, and victorious Russian, Garry Kasparov. While this independent move was seen as a publicity stunt to help the poorly attended contest, her real reason displays her generous heart. 'I went because no public figure had been there to say to Nigel: "Well done, we're so proud of you." When I told him his face lit up,' she said to friends afterwards. Diana proved to be no fair-weather ally. By chance Kasparov's manager met her in her gym the following day. He asked if she wanted to meet the Russian champion. 'I'll stick with our boy,' she told him.

There is a kind of wide-eyed innocence about her activities, a spontaneity matched only by the cynicism of her enemies in the press and Palace. Her determination to break free from official advice and rely on her own instincts means that from time to time her naivety is cruelly exposed. 'I would never describe her as streetwise,' is a frequent comment made by her circle. She demonstrated her simplistic approach when she met the Prime Minister to talk about her ambition to be a roving ambassador for Britain, focusing particularly on humanitarian issues.

Her belief is that conflicts are continued unnecessarily because pride, usually male, stalls communications. Diana's solution was to provide a softer, feminine approach, using her sensitivity and intuition to help unblock choked lines of discussion. Innocent certainly, grandiose possibly, but the notion of the princess acting as a humanitarian ambassadress did win an enthusiastic response from the Prime Minister. Unfortunately, her tactic of bypassing the Palace rather backfired.

The Prime Minister referred the proposal—with his hearty endorsement—to Buckingham Palace for their consideration, who politely informed Downing Street that this was the kind of role tailor-made for the Prince of Wales. 'We want the heir not her' was the all too familiar cry from the Palace, effectively ending her dreams. While she moaned about the Prime Minister's gullibility in consulting the Palace, she failed to see that, under the circumstances, he was duty-bound to proceed in that manner. Her naivety was exposed once more when two young boys were killed by an IRA bomb planted in Warrington town centre. She phoned both sets of parents to express her sadness and sympathy, but her surprise intervention in April 1993 came shortly after Buckingham Palace announced that the Duke of Edinburgh would represent the royal family at the memorial service. She told Wendy Parry, mother of bomb victim Tim, that she would dearly love to hug and comfort her at the service. 'I really want to be there but I can't be,' she said. 'My father-in-law is coming instead.' The call to the Parry home at Great Sankey, Warrington came at six o'clock in the evening just minutes before a crew from Sky TV arrived to broadcast a live interview.

The Parrys' innocent disclosure of the royal call merely added fuel to the flames of controversy surrounding relations between the princess and the Palace. Even though Diana had left her diary empty to attend the service, the Palace made it clear that the duke, not hitherto known for his compassion, was the 'appropriate choice'. The princess was mortified that her phone call of sympathy had deflected attention from the memorial service itself. Ironically she decided not to send a note of sympathy because in the past they have been sold or given to newspapers by the victims themselves. As the princess admitted: 'It was a monumental cock-up. I really had my wrists slapped.' Although her attempt to demonstrate that she could run her own life badly backfired, she was insistent that she should continue to control her public life. 'I know that I will make blunders,' she remarked to an aide. 'There is so much that I have missed out on. I have a lot of growing up to do.'

During a long summer break, which sat uneasily with her public protestations of frugality, such as travelling economy class on foreign visits, Diana tried to come to terms with her new life. As one of Diana's closest advisers explained:

Diana is on a voyage of discovery at the moment. What we are seeing is her real personality coming through because she is no longer bound so much by the royal system. People in authority, be it journalists, politicians or courtiers, find it hard to handle her spontaneity, her vitality and energy as well as her genuine affection for people. They will always try and interpret her behaviour as manipulative and unsuitable. Certainly her timing will be off occasionally but you have to remember that she married young and has conformed to an image for the last decade that is not her. She will make mistakes, but ultimately we will see a genuine manifestation of the real person.

Throughout her royal career, the Princess of Wales has preferred to show her true persona in private trips to hospices, cancer wards and her other charities. Dismayed that her every public appearance was routinely channelled into the 'Charles versus Diana' scenario, she had for many months been secretly exploring royal visits that brought her as close to the people as possible without the need for the bemedalled flunkeys, the smiling officials, the ladies in new hats and the ubiquitous photographers. During the summer of 1992, when public attention on her marriage was at its most intense, she had begun a series of 'awaydays' to hospices, visiting institutions in Blackpool and Hull to comfort the diseased and the dying. 'I would do this full-time if I could,' she told a friend. 'I don't find it at all exhausting.' She visited refuges for battered women, shelters for the homeless, entertained charity officials at Kensington Palace and joined them for a variety of discussion groups.

During one seminar towards the end of 1992, with Relate, the marriage guidance agency, officials discussed the problems of their long waiting list as unhappy couples awaited advice. When she suggested making a video of general guidance, she was thrilled by the enthusiastic response from administrators. She is so used to being judged for her beauty and style rather than her ideas and common sense that when she wins approval for her brains she reacts with a kind of shocked surprise. In this way her speech-making occupies a central place in her royal persona. Again, it forces the media and the public to judge her for what she says rather than how she looks.

At first, like most people, she was absolutely petrified of speaking in public; now she rather enjoys the challenge. It was no coincidence that she chose a speech to announce her withdrawal from public life. Nothing gives her greater delight than acknowledgment for a well-crafted and delivered speech. 'Jeffrey Archer would be proud of that,' her private secretary Patrick Jephson told her as she rehearsed one speech before leaving Kensington Palace. The act of standing before an audience and, for a few minutes, directing and controlling their thinking was nerve-wracking, but ultimately satisfying. While she acknowledged that she had a poor speaking voice, which lacked projection, Diana, at heart a very competitive person, was determined to polish her performance. Initially she enlisted the help of film director Richard

Attenborough and later her friend, actor Terence Stamp, for general advice. Her first speeches, though hesitant, gradually earned her praise and recognition. One of the proudest moments in her royal career was when she was given an award by Evian, the bottled water company, for a speech where she expanded on the need for nurturing children in society. Academics at Harvard University were impressed and invited her to make a short lecture tour of the States dealing with the issue of violence in the home.

Flattered but apprehensive, she decided that she should hone her embryonic skills. Her fitness teacher at the time, Carol Ann Brown, recommended her own voice coach, Peter Settelen, who had helped her when she recorded a fitness video. Their first meeting at Kensington Palace in September 1993 was the start of a fruitful relationship between the princess and the former star of the TV soap Coronation Street. It was not simply a case of helping her breathing and pronunciation, but Settelen wrote ten speeches, helping the princess to marshall her thoughts and craft an argument. While his sympathetic, 'New-Age' philosophy struck a responsive chord with the princess, at times she was faced with an unsympathetic audience. She was upset when the Agony Aunt Claire Rayner accused her of 'glamorizing' eating disorders when Diana described bulimia as a 'shameful friend' and talked about 'the spiral of despair' provoked by bulimia and anorexia nervosa. While her delivery was measured and authoritative, her sentiments provoked a hostile reaction. 'You do not show a princess who has the benefit of the best of everything and say here's an example of someone with this problem,' complained Rayner, a view which earned much support.

The princess was all the more shocked because, as she admitted afterwards, even as she made the speech she felt moved by her own words. Worse was to follow. 'I am fed up with Diana's self-indulgent psychobabble,' wrote the conservative Catholic columnist Mary Kenny in June, twenty-four hours after Diana made a speech on the dangers for women of dependence on tranquilizers and other drugs, which turned them into 'depressed zombies'. Diana told a Turning Point conference: 'These pills, these mother's little helpers, have left a legacy of millions of women locked into a terrible torment, doomed to a life of dependence from which there is still very little help to escape.' She continued: 'If we, as a society, continue to disable women by encouraging them to believe they should only do things that are thought to benefit their family . . . if they feel they never have the right to anything that is just for themselves . . . then they will live only in the shadow of others . . . But if we can help give them back their right to fulfil their own potential . . . maybe fewer women would find themselves living a life that is bleak beyond belief.'

Mary Kenny, an acerbic commentator, was unimpressed, her acid comments cutting the princess far more deeply than perhaps she had intended. She argued: 'Princess Diana has come to maturity in a modern world of Californian psychobabble, in which people identify themselves as victims needing "support" at every turn. It is a world which demands happiness and fulfilment as a "right" and looks for baddies to "blame" if happiness and fulfilment are not forthcoming.' Kenny denounced the theory that women were poor, helpless and passive victims of society, contending: 'Don't let's hang on every word of Princess Di's when she underlines the "poor little me" syndrome for women, or tells us piteously that we are all victims . . . Women are strong individuals and we should affirm that, not this culture of victimhood and complaint.'

The princess read and reread the article, stunned by the ferocity of the attack. 'Do I really talk psychobabble? What am I doing wrong?' she asked her advisers plaintively. Kenny's cutting criticism hurt her not only because it inadvertently unmasked her own personal psychology of victimhood as well as harshly scrutinizing her developing beliefs, particularly in women's issues, but it also served as a searing indictment of the new direction of her public life, namely her speechmaking. For years she had been celebrated simply for being. Now she wanted to be judged for doing, in words and deeds: AIDS, battered women, drug addiction, alienation and loneliness are challenging causes, not only for herself but also society. She was learning the hard way that this was a school of hard knocks. Just to rub it in, that summer the invitation to address Harvard students and make the prestigious Dimbleby lecture were withdrawn. The American university was annoyed that the news of the lecture tour was prematurely leaked; in her excitement the princess had informed numerous friends. As one courtier silkily observed: 'Maybe this will teach her a lesson.'

That was one of many low points in a miserable summer. Confused by the hostility of the media which once lauded her, battered by the Palace machine and constantly looking over her shoulder at Prince Charles's camp, the princess was at the end of her tether. She had started the year enthusiastically and energetically, but as the months went by the carping and the criticism, both inside and outside the Palace, wore down her spirit. It showed in her stale response to bread-and-butter royal duties. Even though she noticed that the complexion of the crowds had changed—'It's no longer little old ladies and children but my generation,' she said proudly. The continual round of handshaking, tree-planting, small talk and smaller children was, to her mind, both repetitive and pointless. 'She turned on the smile and shook hands without any real interest in what was going on,' observed a friend. At the end of June the princess decided that her 'awaydays', her visits outside London, should end. Diana vented her frustration on her staff, loudly complaining if they added extra events or altered schedules. 'I'm the biggest prostitute in the world,' she moaned to a friend. 'I'm handed round like a tube of Smarties.' The day she took part in a photo call during her July visit to Zimbabwe, where she was pictured doling out food to children like a glorified waitress, symbolized her deep dissatisfaction with the whole inane circus. She felt the exercise humiliated her, patronized the children, and demeaned the purpose of her visit, by reinforcing the 'begging-bowl' image of Africa. For what? So that Fleet Street could send home a clichéd picture of the Princess of Wales in Africa. She vowed that it would never happen again.

The draining visit to Africa, the cumulative stresses and strains of the last year, as well as the underlying misery of her royal life, had taken their toll. Introspective and depressed, the princess found herself crying for no reason, worrying continually about Prince Charles, the papers and the Palace. On one occasion she was seen, looking lost, forlorn and red-eyed, at the juice bar of her health club. Her friend, Catherine Soames, rushed over to Kensington Palace to give Diana a stern talking to during one long bout of tears. Then the Duchess of York rang to say that her psychics had forecast that the princess would be in tears for at least two weeks. No reason was given, but their predictions proved accurate.

Diana's normally robust health suffered, exacerbated by her inability to sleep. When homeopathic sleeping draughts failed, she called in a sleep therapist who measured and regulated her oxygen intake during the night. Headaches, caused by stress, dogged many waking hours. In desperation she was put in touch with a nun who practised the 'mind over body' techniques advanced by the American, Louise Hay, in an effort to relieve her inner tension. It became an effort just to leave Kensington Palace. On several occasions her homeopathic doctor, Mary Loveday, would be summoned at short notice from her Harley Street practice to give the appropriate medication to help her face the day, especially when she knew she had to endure a tough round of public engagements. Her private misery showed in public anger. 'You make my life hell,' she shouted at photographer, Keith Butler, when he snapped her and the children as they left a West End cinema. She prodded his chest and jabbed her finger in his face before stalking back to William and Harry.

She needed a holiday, but even that dream rapidly turned into a nightmare. Diana flew first to Bali with friends and then joined her boys at Disney World in Florida. Palace courtiers strongly disapproved, fearing that it would degenerate into a media-circus. They suggested the privacy of Balmoral but Diana ignored their advice, reasoning that, as Princess Anne had taken her children to Florida the previous year, there should be few problems. In the event, the party was hounded by paparazzi. The phrase 'We told you so' hung in the air when she returned to Kensington Palace. However, Diana had had time to ponder her future, and had come to the conclusion that if she wanted to conserve her health and sanity, she had to organize her life in a radically different way.

Returning from holiday, which cost an estimated £30,000, she was greeted with the tabloid banner headlines branding her a 'hypocrite' for taking an expensive holiday while heading charities for the starving. More worrying, Prince Charles had hired two public relations executives to spearhead his campaign of rehabilitation. Then the Palace delivered the coup de grâce. She was informed that Alexandra 'Tiggy' Legge-Bourke had been hired by Prince Charles to be William and Harry's companion when they were with their father.

The wolves were circling for the kill. Her enemies had undermined her status, her personality and her position. Now they wanted the one thing in her life she held most dear, her motherhood.

'When,' she plaintively asked, 'will I get out of this hellhole?'

5

'My Acting Career Is Over'

OVER THE PAST FEW DAYS she had steeled herself for this moment. 'I am not going to cry,' she told herself over and over again, 'I am not going to cry.' When the novelist Jeffrey Archer asked her if she would be able to control her emotions she was resolute. There would be no tears. She was determined that her withdrawal from public life would be carried out with propriety and professionalism.

The scene was her drawing room at Kensington Palace, the time 10.30am on Friday 3 December 1993. Almost a year had passed since the official separation of the Prince and Princess of Wales. Final preparation for the speech she was due to make was taking place, as the princess and the best-selling author discussed the mechanics for the latest chapter of the saga of the princess's relations with the Palace, the press and her public. Just twenty-four hours before, Archer had simply been a minor character in a humdrum royal drama, a master of ceremonies at a charity luncheon, in aid of Headway National Head Injuries Association, where Diana was to be guest of honour. Now he was central to the execution of the story.

On Thursday afternoon the political impresario had received two urgent phone calls: one from Captain Edward Musto, Diana's equerry, requesting his presence at Kensington Palace the following morning, the other from Downing Street, asking him to attend a private meeting that evening with the Prime Minister's principal private secretary, Alex Allan. When he arrived at Number 10, Archer was told that the text of the princess's speech was being altered to include a statement about her future role. The novelist was asked explicitly not to make any suggestions or alterations, 'not a word more, not a word less'. He was asked if he could help the princess get through her ordeal.

Just twelve hours later he was seated on a sofa in her drawing room, his half-moon glasses perched on the end of his nose, silently reading the three-page statement. Her speech had obviously been rewritten several times and was almost in the form of a legal document, the text having been agreed by the Queen and Prime Minister beforehand. None the less, it was a poignant testament and Archer wondered aloud if the princess would really be able to cope.

In spite of her reassurances, Archer knew that changes to the charity lunch must be made if Diana was to effect a dignified departure. The event, in London's Hilton Hotel, had been scheduled to have three speakers and a charity auction, as well as the princess's speech. Predicting the pandemonium that would ensue following her farewell statement, he decided shrewdly to convince the other speakers not to give their speeches but concentrate on the auction so at least the charity could raise much-needed cash. He would then offer the floor to the princess, after which she could be whisked away to Kensington Palace in a waiting royal limousine.

His instincts proved sound. The atmosphere was electric, the media expectant and the princess nervous, her hands visibly shaking as she picked at a salad of avocado, tomato and mozzarella cheese. The princess kept an eye on the master of ceremonies to make sure all was running to plan. At the appropriate moment she walked to the podium. Then, in a sometimes quavering, yet defiant voice, she appealed for 'time and space' after more than a decade in the spotlight. During her five-minute speech she spoke of the unrelenting media exposure, and while she singled out the Queen and Duke of Edinburgh for their 'kindness and support' Diana never once mentioned her estranged husband.

When I started my public life twelve years ago, I understood that the media might be interested in what I did. I realized then that their attention would inevitably focus on both our private and public lives. But I was not aware of how overwhelming that attention would become; nor the extent to which it would affect both my public duties and my personal life, in a manner that has been hard to bear.

Indicating that she would continue to support a small number of charities while she set about rebuilding her private life, the princess emphasized:

My first priority will continue to be our children, William and Harry, who deserve as much love, care and attention as I am able to give, as well as an appreciation of the tradition into which they were born.

After a forty-five-second thank-you speech by Jeffrey Archer, the princess left the Grand Ballroom to an emotional standing ovation.

When she reached the relative sanctity of Kensington Palace, Diana was relieved, saddened, but quietly elated. 'For the first time in twelve years with this family I have been allowed to do something on my own. I wanted to do it my way and I did,' she said. 'Now I can cry.' For once she knew that she had support. Earlier in the week she had seen the Queen and Prince Philip at Buckingham Palace to finalize arrangements. While they had asked her if she would still attend State occasions—the answer was a polite 'no'—they were understanding of her position. The night before she took centre stage, Prime Minister John Major had taken time off from the Anglo-Irish summit discussions in Dublin to wish her well. Her boys William and Harry were ecstatic. 'Oh mummy, what a relief,' they choroused when she told them her news.

Only her husband had struck a discordant note. 'It's been a hell of a battle because Prince Charles has hit the roof,' she told a friend. 'Charles has been whingeing that he wants the stage on his own and now he has got it,' she added bitterly. The princess was unequivocal about who was to blame for her premature departure from public life. 'My husband's side have made my life hell for the last year.'

The dramatic way she left the stage emphasized her growing estrangement from the royal system. Traditionally the Buckingham Palace press office would have been entrusted with such a statement. Yet minutes before she got to her feet, royal officials were unaware of the exact nature of her sentiments. The manner, the timing and the delivery were all hers, a graphic demonstration of her growing emancipation. She was delighted that her decision had been kept secret for six weeks, she was proud of the way she had handled the endless objections from the Queen, the Prime Minister, Prince Charles and a procession of courtiers, and she was exhilarated that she had been able to cope on such an emotive occasion without breaking down.

The timing, however, owed as much to her astrologer as it did to the royal calendar. Ostensibly, the princess had decided to step down before her usual planning meeting, where her visits for the next four months are decided, so as not to inconvenience her 118 charities. However, those close to Diana believe that the royal soothsayer was just as important. The astrologer had indicated that early December would be a propitious time for the princess to make decisive changes in her life.

Ironically, the princess was troubled less by her decision about retiring from public life, than she was about how to handle the men in her life. Her growing estrangement from Inspector Ken Wharfe, her long-serving, long-suffering close protection officer, was a constant source of vexation; she was paranoid about losing her trusted staff; and the future actions of Prince Charles occupied many hours of discussion.

Her relations with the police were complex and contradictory. Throughout her royal career she had found their presence irksome. Little things annoyed her. She couldn't play music in the car as loud as she liked, she always had to inform them where she was going, and she knew that some of her friends found her shadow inhibiting. However, over the years she had accepted that they were a necessary nuisance; indeed sometimes she was grateful to have them around. For example, when she was shopping in Kensington High Street one morning with the boys, she suddenly found herself surrounded by photographers. The boys, particularly William, were upset while she was furious but helpless. So she was delighted when her bodyguards promptly cleared the way, stopped the traffic and allowed her to make her escape for a private lunch date. For their part, the police tried to be sensitive to Diana and keep a low profile.

At the same time, she formed strong bonds with her bodyguards, thanks to her upbringing, her innate generosity and her loneliness. It was no coincidence that Diana went to see the Kevin Costner movie, *The Bodyguard*, as soon as it was released in Britain. She remembers their birthdays, buys them presents like cashmere jumpers or shirts from Turnbull & Asser, the fashionable Jermyn Street store, and sends notes to their wives if she keeps them out late. 'My father said treat everybody as an individual and never throw your weight around,' she says. 'I was brought up to look after others.' It is a trait she has passed on to her sons. They happily fetch and carry for her bodyguards, even waiting at tables at informal occasions. Diana's considerate nature was fully expressed when she discovered that her bodyguard, Chief Inspector Graham 'Smudger' Smith, was suffering from cancer. She invited him and his wife Eunice to join her on a Mediterranean cruise. In May 1993 as his life was drawing to a close, she visited him several times at a hospice in Esher, Surrey. At her express insistence he was transferred from an open public ward to a private room, knowing that the popular but modest policeman would never have been so forward. Following his death she comforted his wife and insisted on attending his funeral at the expense of her public duties.

For their part, her police officers used to keep the media at bay, tell her the latest Palace gossip, cover her tracks and keep her supplied with risqué jokes. Yet her relationship with her bodyguards was more than an extravagant display of good manners. Over the years several of her Scotland Yard minders have become father figures to her, listening to her problems and giving down-to-earth advice. They became firm allies in her battle with her husband and the Palace, friendly faces in a hostile world.

There is, for example, still a special place in her heart for Inspector Barry Mannakee. Every year in late spring, usually May, she makes a secret pilgrimage to the City of London Crematorium at Redbridge, where his ashes are scattered. The princess, disguised with an oversized head scarf, stands in silent tribute to a man who was a true friend when she felt lost and alone in the royal system. He was by her side during the mid-1980s when her relationship with Prince Charles was rapidly disintegrating. Her closeness to Mannakee provoked jealousy among fellow officers and anger from the prince, who was instrumental in having him transferred to other duties. Less than a year after his departure in July 1986, he was killed in a motorcycle accident near his home in Loughton, Essex. When she received the news on her car phone, while she and Prince Charles were travelling to

Heathrow and on to the Cannes film festival in May the following year, the princess was devastated. For a long time she believed that MI5, the security service, was involved in his death, although she is now satisfied that his death was an accident. His departure and subsequent death was a dreadful loss at a time when she was in what she calls 'the dark ages' of her marriage and royal life, her unhappiness and despair at their most intense. Since then she has used a clairvoyant to try and contact Mannakee and dead family relatives, particularly her uncle, Lord Fermoy, who committed suicide, and her much-loved grandmother, Cynthia Spencer. She has told friends that Mannakee 'meant an awful lot to me. He was my father figure and looked after me.'

The psychology of her relationship with some of her bodyguards was intricate and conflicting. On the one hand a father/daughter relationship, but it could also be one of employer and employee, the police officer being reminded he was employed to do her bidding. Therefore she could be both distant and businesslike, or friendly and confiding within a short period of time. Her attitude could be difficult for her bodyguards to predict and deal with. She projects an air of vulnerability, which makes most men instinctively want to protect her. It is a beguiling but deceptive quality, as those who wish to defend her soon find. 'She encourages familiarity but once someone gets too close she shuts down, terrified that when you really get to know her there is less there than meets the eye,' notes a friend. Far from being a doe-like innocent, the princess is a young woman who wants to be in control, both in her public and private life. So it was annoying, not to say humiliating, for her that the men with whom she was in constant contact, her bodyguards, ultimately had the right to take physical command of her life. 'The good thing about guarding a woman is that if the worst happens, you can always throw her over your shoulder and run for it,' one of her former bodyguards told new recruits. Diana came to resent this image of the powerful Tarzan, protecting the helpless Jane, and for months argued that a female police officer be assigned to her. In April 1993 she got her wish when Sergeant Carol Quirk joined her team.

Add to this her growing suspicion that police agents were acting for the Palace and it is plain to see why her bodyguard Ken Wharfe felt that he was treading on eggshells throughout 1993. The first signs came during her holiday to the Caribbean in January with the boys. There was a *frisson* of motherly jealousy when William and Harry insisted on joining Ken for games of cricket on the beach or meals at the Montpelier Hotel in Nevis. What was once seen as fatherly concern was now interpreted as overfamiliarity.

At home there were tiffs about little things. One morning they were on a shopping session in Kensington when he warned her against parking near where three cars were already wheel-clamped. Voices were raised and eventually Diana abruptly got out of the car and stalked into a nearby music store. For forty minutes her policeman waited patiently for her to return, knowing that she had stormed off without any money. On another occasion, it was his turn to be both angry and embarrassed when, without his knowledge, she had her rooms at Kensington Palace swept for bugs. Not only did it imply a lack of trust in the Metropolitan Police, but a lack of confidence in her chief bodyguard.

The chill really set in during Diana's prolonged summer holidays in 1993. Several days before the princess departed for Florida, her police officer was planning his own reconnaissance of Disney World. Wharfe and Diana had discussed the likelihood of media interest. He felt that by travelling under an assumed name—usual operational practice—Fleet Street would be unable to follow the royal scent. 'Don't worry,' she told him, 'they already know.' Puzzled by her foreknowledge, he arrived at his hotel to discover that royal reporter, Richard Kay, was already there. The only conclusion was that the princess or someone very close to her had alerted selected journalists about her plans. It was alarming as it corroded the bond of trust between the princess and her shadow.

When the party left the bustle of Florida for the quieter waters of Kate Menzies' holiday home at Lyford Key in the Bahamas, the royal bodyguards endured a frosty welcome. Extra police officers had been flown out, and the princess, already tetchy about the existing police presence, was concerned about the cost to the taxpayer. They agreed to keep a low profile, basing themselves in nearby quarters. So the princess was not best pleased when her sons, far from ignoring their company, joined them for meals and games. On the way home, as the bodyguard team were about to leave for the airport, the princess insisted on taking the boys for a gentle walkabout to thank everyone for making her stay pleasant and enjoyable. Unfortunately her gesture delayed the plane and angered her police officers. On the flight back to Britain the distance between Wharfe and Diana was evident to the journalists travelling with them. 'The magic has gone,' Wharfe told acquaintances and the princess soon heard rumours that he was angling for a new post, possibly in America.

She discussed her worries with the Duchess of York who sympathized. She too had felt uncomfortable with the constant police presence. There were deeper springs to Diana's discontent. The police were used as scapegoats for the continual frustration she felt inside the royal system. They were a visible symbol of her perceived imprisonment. Her estrangement from Wharfe and her belief that she could organize her own life merely confirmed her decision to reduce or leave behind her police guard when she retired from public life.

A confrontation between the princess and her senior bodyguard was inevitable. Early in October the princess was told about off-the-cuff remarks Wharfe had allegedly made about his royal boss to the effect that she needed a good smack across her backside. Diana was indignant. While she dreaded a showdown with Wharfe, she realized that it was necessary to clear the air. He vigorously denied the accusation but the damage was done. Following their encounter at Kensington Palace, the princess had several formal discussions with Prince Charles's bodyguard, Chief Inspector Colin Trimming, who was in charge of all the royal close protection officers. They not only discussed Wharfe's future, but also scaling down the police presence around her. It was decided that it would be best for all concerned to have a parting of the ways.

In early November the princess and her shadow had a friendly farewell meeting in her drawing room at Kensington Palace, where she presented him with a carriage clock and thanked him for seven years' loyal service. It was noticeable, however, that Inspector Wharfe, who is now responsible for protecting visiting VIPs, was missing when the princess entertained the rest of her police protection team for a farewell dinner at the Savoy Hotel in February 1994.

As an ironic counterpoint, just as Diana was discussing with her aides ways of dispensing with Wharfe's services, Prince Charles's camp suspected her policeman of orchestrating her publicity campaign. They believed that Wharfe was the mastermind behind photo opportunities with Diana and the boys at various locations: on a Caribbean beach, on the ski slopes at Lech in Austria and at Thorpe Park amusement park in Britain. Nothing could be further from the truth; in the absence of a press officer, he had been merely keeping the peace between the princess and photographers. Wharfe was another honourable victim of the suspicion and rivalry between the two camps.

At a time when Diana was quietly working on a new direction in her life, she craved calm in her public life and the support of trusted allies in private. It was not to be. The departure of Wharfe had an unsettling effect on her staff. They felt the first ripples of a major change in her way of life, and they were worried.

It was a routine evening on Monday 1 November 1993 as Diana left Kensington Palace for a charity event—a show by the Chicken Shed Theatre Company at Leicester Square's Equinox playhouse. As she and her lady-in-waiting, Mrs Jean Pike, were about to leave, her butler, Paul Burrell, handed her a letter. Like a grenade without a pin, it had been gingerly passed around all day between her private secretary, equerry and bodyguard. Its contents exploded in Diana's face on the way to the theatre, where 250 mentally and physically handicapped youngsters were waiting eagerly to greet her.

Her chauffeur, Simon Solari, who had provided amusing and loyal company over the last difficult twelve months, had sent her his resignation. He planned to join Prince Charles's staff as the number-two driver. (The personable Solari was later promoted to the prince's valet.) As she reread the letter, she was not sure what hurt most—the fact that he had remained silent about his decision or that he was joining the 'enemy' camp. Something inside her just snapped and Diana burst into floods of tears. 'It hit me when I was least expecting it and so all the rest of the stuff came up,' she told friends.

His decision could not have come at a worse time. An hour before, she had just said her private farewells to her friend Lucia Flecha de Lima who was leaving London for Washington where her husband, the Brazilian ambassador, was to take up a new post. She had also spoken to the Foreign Secretary, Douglas Hurd, to apologize for a premature newspaper leak about a proposed visit to Moscow later that month. To cap it all the trip, which she called 'very grown up', had been postponed because the Russian president, Boris Yeltsin, had called elections. Still reeling from a particularly tense and difficult meeting with Prince Charles a couple of days before, suddenly she broke down. With tears streaming down her face, they parked by the Serpentine lake in Hyde Park so that she could regain her composure. The princess arrived at the engagement, red-eyed and distracted. Just thirty minutes later she abruptly departed, her aides claiming that she had a migraine headache. In the privacy of her rooms she cried her eyes out, despairing that she would ever be able to live her life without constant crisis.

The following morning she had regained sufficient composure to speak to Simon in her private sitting room. Rather nervously, he explained that he had to think of his family as he planned his future. The princess was understanding, wishing him well in his new job and accepting one month's notice. Her staff were as shocked as she was by Solari's decision. In a touching gesture her dresser, Helena Roach, who previously informed the princess that she had planned to leave, told her that she would stay for the moment to show solidarity.

By lunchtime, following a two-hour chat with business motivator guru, Anthony Robbins, she was back on form, chortling over a pointed sentence in the London *Evening Standard*'s report of her public breakdown which said: 'Migraine has not figured largely in the princess's list of psychologically related ailments.' In fact stress headaches are the bane of her life, although she has never suffered from migraines. She even managed a jokey speech about her well-being following comments by her step-grandmother, Dame Barbara Cartland, that her bulimia nervosa had taken hold once again. When she arrived at a lunch in aid of the WellBeing charity later that week she told a much-amused audience: 'Ladies and gentlemen, you are very lucky to have your patron here today. I was supposed to have my head down the loo for most of the day. I am supposed to be dragged off the minute I leave here by men in white coats, but if it's all right with you I thought I might postpone my nervous breakdown for a more appropriate moment. It is amazing what a migraine can bring on.' In reality, for the last few years, she has controlled her bulimia using the American drug, Prozac, dubbed 'liquid sunshine' because of its effectiveness as an anti-depressant. Her use of this controversial 'wonder drug', which has been suspected of causing bouts of violent anger and mood swings in some patients, has meant that her bulimia has been under control for some time. The fact that she no longer attends private royal gatherings that used to generate attacks of bulimia also helps.

Other painful journeys in to her unhappy past have taken place with Susie Orbach, the psychotherapist and author of seven books, including *Fat Is a Feminist Issue*. Diana has had numerous consultations with Orbach over the past year, which, though inevitably traumatic, demonstrate Diana's determination to confront her past. She drives herself to therapy, joking with builders working outside as she goes in and out of Orbach's north London house.

A consultation with her soothsayer greatly unsettled her. She predicted that two weeks after the full moon, which was due to fall on 30 October, Prince Charles would face a major upset in his life.

Diana's oracle gave the date of Saturday 13 November—the day before Charles's forty-fifth birthday—as the turning point in his life. It was the time when he would give up the Crown he coveted, possibly for the woman he loved, Camilla Parker Bowles. There was more. It was forecast that at the same time Prince William would be forced to take on a grave and onerous responsibility. The obvious conclusion was that Prince Charles planned to step aside for his son, Prince William, and allow him to become the next king so that he could marry Camilla. It was heady stuff. For a time it dominated Diana's thinking and paralysed her actions as she counted the days. 'He is going to hit the sandbanks,' she told friends, 'his ship is going to sink.'

The royal oracle proved reliable, but only in the world of make-believe. As the soothsayer and Diana pondered the prince's future, on television a Prime Minister was plotting the downfall of a king, who bore an uncanny resemblance to Charles in both attitude and mannerisms, and replacing him with the son of his estranged wife, a blonde who looked remarkably like Diana. The television version of Michael Dobbs's book *To Play the King* fascinated the princess not least because it dealt with issues so close to home. 'Don't we describe someone like Dobbs as a visionary?' commented the princess light-heartedly.

Bizarrely, a Russian zealot predicted that the same day, 13 November, would bring the end of the world, but, in the end, the day passed much like any other. However, a couple of weeks later the prince did find himself mired in further speculation about his future. His complaints in the *Financial Times* that the Government failed to utilize his talents on his overseas tours were taken so seriously by the Prime Minister that it was discussed in Cabinet. However, it was left to the Archdeacon of York to light the blue touch-paper of debate about whether the prince was fit to be king because of his alleged relationship with Camilla Parker Bowles. 'My view would be that Charles made solemn vows before God in church about his marriage, and it seems . . . that he began to break them almost immediately. He has broken his trust and vow to God on one thing. How can he then go into Westminster Abbey and take the coronation vows?' The churchman's comments on the BBC *Today* radio programme sparked an instant debate, replete with phone-ins, opinion polls and howls of anger from the prince's camp. His friend and former equerry, Nicholas Soames MP, waded in: 'It's wounding and hurtful. [The prince] will inherit the throne, that is the end of the matter,' he said, his comments endorsed by a familiar cast of Establishment characters. The public was not impressed. Opinion polls regularly showed more support for William than Prince Charles as the next sovereign.

During the Prince and Princess of Wales's formal meeting in the last week of October, they had discussed two things: Diana's future plans and their divorce. The prince was tetchy and ill-tempered, and their relationship, already jagged and awkward, deteriorated further. Armed with the knowledge of Diana's future plans, Charles attempted to pre-empt any backlash by complaining to the *Financial Times* that his serious public role was submerged beneath speculation about his marriage. For the last few months their only communication had been via memos that had sailed back and forth about Christmas arrangements for the boys and the royal train. Charles felt the private train was his 'perk' and discouraged the princess from travelling on it, which goes some of the way to explain why, when she visited Wales to support the national rugby team and take the boys on a semi-official visit, she travelled in an ordinary British Rail carriage. The mood of the meeting was not helped when the prince broached the subject of divorce. They had previously discussed 'the D word' on the telephone. Charles was eager for a decision. The princess, acting on the advice of her lawyer Lord Mishcon, made it clear that she was happy to wait, secure in her Palace redoubt. That reply did not please the prince who was inclined to settle the issue once and for all. Her proposed retirement simply muddied the waters.

Problems with the prince, the Palace, the police, the press and the paparazzi were now her daily diet. An incident a few days earlier was particularly upsetting. When she took the boys to see the West End musical *Grease* at the Dominion theatre the party found themselves surrounded by black-jacketed cameramen. The boys were alarmed and upset. 'It was horrid,' she told a friend. 'You would think they had never seen me before. They climbed over cars and jumped over the children. These were grown men.' It was the latest in a never-ending series of ill-tempered spats with professional cameramen.

Yet it was an amateur photographer who finally settled her decision about public life once and for all. If she had been hesitant before, her mind was made up when she looked at the front page of the *Sunday Mirror* early in November and saw a full-page picture of herself working out at her former health club. She had long suspected that these photographs existed but it was still a shock to see herself, dressed in a leotard, exploited in this way.

The gym's manager, New Zealand businessman Bryce Taylor, explained that he had secretly taken the pictures of club member 753 with a hidden £2,500 camera secreted in a box directly above a leg-press machine where Diana regularly worked out. Buckingham Palace, Members of Parliament, other newspaper editors and Lord McGregor, chairman of the Press Complaints Commission, lined up to accuse Mirror Group Newspapers, who had paid a reported £100,000 for the pictures, of a flagrant breach of the princess's privacy. The princess herself felt betrayed and violated. 'Bryce Taylor pushed me into the decision to go,' she remarked later. 'The pictures were horrid, simply horrid.'

She was further infuriated when Taylor had the gall to claim that she secretly wanted the pictures taken. Even though his argument was patently specious, such was the hostility towards the princess among the Establishment, that several influential newspaper columnists and politicians felt there was a grain of truth in his accusations of manipulation. The fact that she had taken the rare step of instructing her lawyers to sue Taylor and Mirror Group Newspapers did not still the critics. (That action is still pending.) It was a further signal to the princess that, however hard she tried, however innocent her actions, a cancer of cynicism was gradually corrupting the public's perception of her position. She had emancipated herself from her marriage, now she was fiercely determined to break free from a gloating media who had for so long held her in their thrall.

For Buckingham Palace courtiers gently trying to entice Diana back into the fold, the 'Peeping-Tom' pictures could not have come at a worse time. All the weapons in their armoury were brought into action. First the big guns were wheeled out. The Queen was understanding. 'Wonderful' was Diana's description of their meeting where she agreed to maintain her links with the Armed Services—she attended the D-Day anniversary services in London and Portsmouth in June 1994—and vowed that she would leave Kensington Palace 'inside six months'. Prince Philip, not normally known for his tact, tried flattery, complimenting her on her forthright decision to take the Daily Mirror and Sunday Mirror to court. 'You're doing well now that you are getting even with the press,' he told her. In late October as the princess was moving inexorably towards a decision, the Prime Minister John Major called in to Kensington Palace for a forty-minute 'tea and sympathy' meeting, where he expressed his personal concern over the difficulty of her position and the unrelenting, often hostile media attention she had faced that autumn.

Then Sir Robert Fellowes and other courtiers went in to bat. They argued that she should prune her charities rather than take an axe to the lot and raised concerns about how she would spend her time now that the boys were away at school. Nor were they happy about the manner in which she wished to withdraw from public life. She was deaf to their entreaties. Their case was not helped when she read a series of newspaper articles on the royal family by

Graham Turner for the *Daily Mail*, which she believed the Palace had inspired, which made condescending remarks about her conduct.

Next came the police, who were extremely reluctant to relinquish authority over her safety. The threat of terrorism, lone madmen and aggressive photographers made her a prime target. She argued, somewhat unrealistically, that, as a semi-private person, she was entitled to live her life the way she wished. As far as she was concerned the same logic applied to her children when they were with her. She believed that, as she felt able to organize private outings in total secrecy, a police presence was unnecessary. Both the Palace and the police were horrified at the very idea of leaving the princes unguarded. The idea could not be tolerated for a moment. While she lost that skirmish, Metropolitan Police chiefs did, with great misgivings, agree to her request that her own personal protection be withdrawn. Their caution was entirely understandable. If anything did happen, they know who would be blamed. Indeed, senior officers at Scotland Yard have already made it clear that they already have their statements prepared if Diana is ever harmed. In fact, since the princess declined to have a formal police presence, the Metropolitan Police has monitored her every move—but from a discreet distance. When she leaves Kensington Palace, she usually informs a member of staff about her destination and the Royal Protection Squad has kept a wary eye on her movements. As a police source said:

'She may think she is on her own, but we still do the best we can to keep an eye on her.'

Finally, there was the reaction from her friends to her decision to retire from public life. Those who knew her best realized that her retirement would give her a much-needed chance to reflect and refocus. If the separation had given her the hope of a new life, her withdrawal from royal duties would give her the opportunity to translate that hope into a vibrant new career, utilizing her undoubted gifts of compassion and caring on a wider, international stage. Others were not so sure. Sir Gordon Reece, a member of the so-called 'Zenda group' who had tried in vain to effect a reconciliation between the prince and princess, had grave doubts. The professional spin doctor had worked part-time for the princess for the last six months, his fees paid by their mutual friend, Lord Palumbo. Just as the Zenda zealots ignored the immutable realities of marriage breakdown in their quixotic quest to bring them together, so Reece misread Diana's serious intent. Reece, who calls Diana 'my child', jokily dismissed her plans. 'Oh, but you are the most famous woman in the world, everyone loves you,' he said, with mock gallantry. The princess cut him short. 'So what,' she replied. The die was now cast. 'It's been a hell of a battle,' she later remarked.

She bowed out, however, to a mixed reception. It was to be expected. When the Queen Mother saw her at Christmas she felt that the princess should have been tougher on the media in her speech. Diana demurred, believing that the subtext of the Queen Mother's remark was intended to indicate that her favourite grandson, Prince Charles, should be absolved of any blame for Diana's departure. As far as Diana was concerned, her estranged husband was the cause of her retirement. Then there were those, like Conservative MP James Hill, who felt that she had made too much of a song and dance act about leaving the Windsor roadshow. 'I think it should have been done a little more quietly,' he argued. 'I don't think there should have been a highly emotional speech which creates the impression that the Princess of Wales has come under pressure from the House of Windsor.'

Many others, even her former enemy John Junor, were moved by her courage in sharing her feelings with her public and at the same time saddened by her loss. He wrote:

My own views of Princess Diana have been the subject of change. But, on one aspect of her character, I have never been in any doubt. She is on the side of the angels. She is a warm, compassionate person who lights up every room she enters. She cares about people. And the people have come to care deeply about her.

The princess was touched by his sentiments and it is typical of her nature that, in the weekend of her retirement, she agreed to make a private visit to see an eleven-year-old girl who was dying of AIDS. Sadly, she passed away only hours before Diana was due to see her.

While Diana expected a hostile reception from her enemies, she was alarmed and not a little angered by a highly charged, three-page fax which arrived on her desk the day after her speech. It was an emotional outpouring from her voice coach and speech writer, Peter Settelen, complaining that he been kept in the dark about her farewell speech. His fervent if rambling memo touched on their personal and professional relationship and made it clear that he felt hurt that she had not asked him to discuss the contents of her speech before she made it. The princess was upset as much by the timing as the sentiments of Settelen's fax and she told him so in her reply. 'The contents of your fax came as an enormous and painful shock at a very difficult time. Forgive me for not attending to it now but I am already in distress and haven't the strength to cope with your misunderstanding of the situation.' When they discussed the issue several days later Settelen explained that, as it was her last speech, he had really wanted to help her prepare for her trial. Once again she was as insistent with her voice coach as she had been with her part-time press officer, the Palace, the police and the royal family. She wanted to do it her way. It is an incident which illustrates once again that the princess was determined to emancipate herself from control, whether this control be benign or malignant. She knew full well that even her allies were pursuing their own agendas, be it self-aggrandizement, social ambition or plain publicity. Everyone wanted a piece of the royal pie, but this princess was no longer on the menu. As she wryly observed: 'Why do I get advised at the beginning and the end, but not in the middle?'

If she needed any convincing that her decision to go was absolutely right for her, it came forty-eight hours after her farewell speech. She spent a reflective, occasionally tearful, weekend trying to relax after the travails of the week. Her osteopath, Michael Skipwith, and masseur, Stephen Twigg, both visited Kensington Palace to help get her into shape for the 'final furlong'—her remaining handful of official engagements. Her first was to join extrovert entrepreneur Richard Branson at Gatwick Airport for the launch of a Virgin Airlines Airbus. It was a media zoo and she was the prize exhibit. She had already turned down his request to wear red—the company signature— and warily anticipated that other surprises might be in store.

They were. As they stood before the aircraft, Diana was serenaded by Chris de Burgh singing 'Lady in Red' and afterwards Branson, in the manner of a winning Formula One racing driver, sprayed a bottle of champagne over the fuselage. As he chatted into a hand-held microphone, he then put his arm around the princess, rather like a game-show host with a reluctant contestant. She may have smiled for the cameras but inside she was counting the seconds until she could escape from this undignified mayhem.

'It was cringe-making,' she told friends afterwards, 'I now know why I'm off.'

A few months later, at a reception at the Serpentine Gallery of which she is patron, the princess was in fine form. She was relaxed, witty and happy amongst friends. The events of 1993 seemed a dim and dismal memory. As she chatted to the movie star Jeremy Irons he told her: 'I've taken a year off acting.'

Diana smiled and replied: 'So have I.'

6

'I Am Going to Be Me'

IT WAS A PERFECT SUMMER'S EVENING as the Princess of Wales prepared to leave her Kensington Palace apartments. Before she walked out of the front door she told her staff that she was going to see her sister Sarah at her Fulham home. Then she drove off on her own in a Ford Scorpio pool car. Her journey did not last long. Minutes later she stopped in Hyde Park where a man was waiting. Casual observers were astonished as her male companion opened the car trunk and climbed in. The princess then quickly sped away from the scene of her secret rendezvous to an unknown destination. 'If Diana is prepared to take a risk like that he must mean a lot to her,' noted one of her closest friends. Several weeks earlier, in April this year, she was spotted by photographers as she drove down Beauchamp Place with a man by her side. As they prepared to pursue, her male companion slid down into his seat, while she catapulted through a set of red traffic lights. They later switched cars and drove off into the night.

Romance and estranged princesses make uneasy bedfellows. Diana knows full well that the road to her future happiness, and possible remarriage, is liberally littered with mantraps. She is acutely aware that her tracks are dogged by the paparazzi, hungry for that jackpot: the first picture of the princess with the new man in her life. The princess's caution is therefore understandable, but, as she admits, 'I can be quite crafty.' She is aware of the turbulence a fresh union would create. Diana once told her husband: 'If I fall in love with somebody else the sparks will fly and God help us.' As Captain James Hewitt, who enjoyed a friendship with the princess until he betrayed her trust by cooperating with a book, admits: 'I think only a few men could cope with the pressure of the attention it would bring.'

However innocent her friendships, she knows from bitter experience that male companions experience weeks, if not years, of misery through the attentions of the media. She has almost lost count of the number of men—and often their wives—who have found themselves front-page news because they have spent a casual evening with her at the cinema, theatre or a restaurant.

As she picks her way towards establishing a new life, the princess is alert to other pitfalls. Even though Charles has admitted his adultery on television, she knows that any liaison she might have that is not carried out discreetly will affect her negotiating position in any future financial settlement. 'His side', she told friends, 'are just waiting to pounce.' Diana was the one who helped the Duchess of York pick up the pieces of her life after the publication of photographs showing her 'financial adviser', John Bryan, sucking her toes in a French holiday villa, and she is determined that she will never make such a mistake.

Timing is vital. If the princess were to remarry, Prince Charles and his family could use the fact as a lever to distance her further from her sons. The Palace would be unwilling to entrust the grooming of the future king to anyone other than his natural parents. Yet the princess, having to a certain extent successfully broken free from her royal life, cannot be denied for ever the chance of finding love in the arms of another man. She eagerly awaits the day when she can share her life in a warm and loving relationship. 'Whoever you are, come here,' she jokes. Her mothering instinct is strong and she has frequently spoken of her longing to have two more children, preferably girls. Indeed, she was intrigued when one astrological forecast predicted a baby this year. She dotes on the Duchess of York's children, Princesses Beatrice and Eugenie, and, in the dying throes of her marriage, often goaded her husband by using them as an example of what he was missing. 'I mobbed him up about them,' she says gleefully. She sees herself marrying a foreigner or at least a man of foreign blood. France appears time and again in her private astrological prophecies both as a future home and the birthplace of the new man in her life. Maybe it is just a coincidence that she is learning French, frequently visits Paris and enjoys private holidays at the Provençal home of her friend, Catherine Soames. As a friend observes: 'She is absolutely hell bent on finding another man at some stage. There is no one in mind but she does have a vision.'

Well-groomed, natty rather than fashionable, Jermyn Street rather than Floral Street, clean-cut, lean and rangy in appearance, well-spoken, courteous and wry in humour are some of the characteristics that appeal to the princess, features which, ironically, many women appreciate in the Prince of Wales. From Adam Russell, Rory Scott and Simon Berry in her teenage years, to William van Straubenzee, Captain James Hewitt, James Gilbey, her voice coach Peter Settelen, masseur Stephen Twigg and reporter Richard Kay—who she has described as 'rather undernourished'—in her adult life, all exhibit to a greater or lesser degree these qualities. It is significant that she is often drawn to men who do not pose a threat, socially, sexually or physically. Yet she is on such friendly terms with the sportsman Will Carling that he arranged for Princes William and Harry to join the

England rugby team for a training-session day at Twickenham in March 1995 only days before the Grand Slam match between England and Scotland.

On the silver screen, she warms to men like the English actor, Tom Conti, for his looks and amusing conversation, as well as Hollywood star, Tom Cruise, for his cheeky sex appeal. She and Kate Menzies went to see the film, *The Firm*, only because Cruise was the principal lead. The actor Terence Stamp, an evergreen sex symbol from the Swinging Sixties, enchants her with his New Age philosophy. At the same time, she is drawn to father figures, men with whom she can flirt in safety because they pose no threat. Men like her benefactor Lord Rothschild, her lawyer Lord Mishcon—she dines with him most weeks—merchant banker, Christopher Balfour, Oliver Hoare and Lords Gowrie and Fawsley have proved susceptible to her undoubted charms—embarrassingly so for middle-aged art dealer, Oliver Hoare. She is very aware of her appeal and the appropriate armoury to employ in the battle of the sexes, calling her high-heeled shoes 'tart's trotters' and her racy red Mercedes sports car 'a tart's dream'. As one elderly peer observes rather wistfully: 'She knows that she has power over men and she knows how to use that to her advantage.' The former French President of France, Valery Giscard d'Estaing, is one of many distinguished elder statesmen to have fallen prey to her 'immense blue eyes, feline movement and lucid and attentive manner.' After one meeting, he gushed, 'You have seen her in the photos and you have thought

The publication of *Diana, Her True Story*, sparked a media-fed furore, which continued unabated until the prince and princess separated in December 1992 (Derrick E. Witty)

Right: Diana kisses William Bartholomew goodbye, watched by his wife, Carolyn. Her visit to their Fulham home came just days after the publication of *Diana, Her True Story*. It was seen by many as an endorsement of the book as Carolyn was one of the named sources (Syndication International)

Below: Since her retirement from public life, the princess has been followed night and day by paparazzi. Without a bodyguard by her side, she is more vulnerable to their often aggressive behaviour. By treating them with unsmiling disdain or hiding her face she hopes that eventually they will leave her alone (Marco Deidda/Alpha)

Facing page: The princess arrives at the fashionable Daphne's restaurant in South Kensington. Even though she is separated, she still wears her wedding and engagement rings (Miguel/Alpha)

Above: The Prince and Princess of Wales deep in conversation at the funeral of her grandmother, Ruth, Lady Fermoy. Diana, feeling ill and tired after a whistle-stop tour of Zimbabwe, sought Charles's opinion on whether she should cancel her two royal engagements that day. Although Charles's advice was to rest, Diana soldiered on to both events (All Action)

Below: The princess with Prince Edward and Lady Sarah Armstrong-Jones at the wedding of Princess Margaret's son, Viscount Linley, to Serena Stanhope. While much was made of Diana's absence from the reception, Diana's explanation was simple: the wedding date had been changed and she already had a previous engagement, to collect her children from their boarding school (Photographers International)

Right: During her four-day tour of Zimbabwe the princess consented to a photo opportunity where she ladled food to hungry youngsters. On further reflection she felt that the whole Palace-inspired exercise was demeaning to both herself and the children, and reinforced the 'begging-bowl' image of Africa (Photographers International)

Below: Diana is a competitive and proficient car driver, so when she had the opportunity to join in this charity go-carting event, the occasion did not stop her from going all-out to win. It gives her a rare chance of being in total control (Terry Hillfry/All Action)

Overleaf: Just weeks after her separation, the princess took her boys for a sunshine holiday on the Caribbean island of Nevis. The pink surfboard was borrowed from the Montpelier Hotel, where she stayed (Nunn Syndication)

The princess and her party in light-hearted mood during their skiing holiday in Lech, Austria. Prince William accidentally tips over a glass of water; the startled princess leaps backwards, and then, good-naturedly, she tries to swipe her giggling son with a napkin. But it is all smiles afterwards (Nunn Syndication)

Left: The princess, her friend Lucia Flecha de Lima and son Antonio, following the graduation ceremony of Lucia's daughter, Beatriz, from Richmond College, held at Kensington Town Hall. Lucia, the wife of the Brazilian ambassador, was much missed by Diana when her husband was transferred from London to Washington
(Dave Chancellor/Alpha)

Below: Diana's butler, Paul Burrell, tries manfully to load the royal car with a handful of helium-filled balloons. Her relationship with her staff is friendly and informal, a far cry from the 'Upstairs Downstairs' world of Buckingham Palace
(Paul Burrell/Rex Features)

The princess leaves St Mary's Hospital, Paddington—where William and Harry were born—after visiting Earl Spencer's son and heir, Louis Frederick John. The elephant motifs on her Escada outfit created jumbo-sized comment and led to accusations that Diana was dressing more like a suburban housewife than a princess (Dave Chancellor/Alpha)

Above: Diana, relaxed and animated, chats with Lord Linley at a London cocktail party. She admires the way Princess Margaret's son has managed to live a relatively normal life even though he is the only man in the land able to call the Queen 'auntie' (Dave Bennett/Alpha)

Left: The princess and her best friends, Kate Menzies and Catherine Soames, discuss their afternoon plans after lunching at San Lorenzo in Knightsbridge (Miguel/Alpha)

Left: Lady in Red . . . the princess returns to her car in Knightsbridge, where she met a *Daily Mail* reporter. She told him she had felt 'raped' by the intrusive paparazzi on her weekend break in Spain. Her conversations with newsman Richard Kay led to accusations that she was 'two-faced', complaining about newspapers one minute, while manipulating them the next (Glenn Harvey)

Below: The casually dressed princess has become a familiar figure in the streets around Kensington and Knightsbridge, while she attempts to lead a normal life without bodyguards and away from the media spotlight (Glenn Harvey)

Above: Lady sees Red . . . Diana is pursued by photographers after a private shopping session goes public. These days she shows no hesitation in running away or hiding from them (Glenn Harvey)

Overleaf: The princess has known London stockbroker William van Straubenzee for many years. When he dated her elder sister Sarah, the teenage Lady Diana Spencer would gladly iron his shirts. From time to time he and the princess have joined the Duke of Roxburghe for weekend house parties at his country estate of Floors Castle in the Scottish Borders (Nunn Syndication)

how pretty she looks but quite simply she is much more beautiful in real life.'

While she is eager to plot a new romantic direction, potential suitors must watch how they conduct themselves. This is a woman who has been sorely hurt by the men who touched her heart and her life. She was rejected by Prince Charles for another woman, her former bodyguard Barry Mannakee was tragically killed, James Gilbey's friendship was cruelly and publicly exposed as a result of Squidgygate, Captain James Hewitt betrayed her in a book, while her relationship with Oliver Hoare stretched his marriage and patience almost beyond endurance. Little wonder, then, that Diana is reluctant to jump aboard the treacherous merry-go-round of romance.

Those men who sit on her sofa at Kensington Palace—and there has been a procession—and declare their undying devotion, adoration and love for the princess are quickly shown the door. 'As soon as they start saying that everyone is madly in love with you, it's instant rejection. It is absolutely repulsive,' she says with feeling. Psychologist, Dr Dennis Friedman, believes that she wants love at a distance, a telephone romance rather than the real thing. More accurately she likes to be in control of a relationship, ditching those who overstep the invisible boundaries of familiarity. She is acutely aware that she is a woman with power over men and she uses her authority to suit herself. As one former beau recalls: 'She can lavish affection on a total stranger and yet shrink back from intimacy with those she knows well. She has a reluctance to reveal herself, as if she is afraid of being found out. Yet she has this aura about her, some people she puts totally at ease, with others she keeps up this front.' While she is in command of her life in a way which was unthinkable even two years ago, a small corner of her heart still longs for a romantic knight in shining armour to whisk her away to a new life. 'Her head tells her that she would like to be the ambassador to the world, her heart tells her that she would like to be wooed by an adoring billionaire,' comments a friend.

Her head and heart may tug in different directions but her face tells the story of her evolving character. The blushing bride, all innocence and eagerness, contrasts vividly with the features of a woman who has experienced the bitterness of betrayal and deceit during the last decade. Commentator William Rees-Mogg described her physiognomy well: 'A nose expressive of powerful will, commanding eyes set in strong sockets. Hers is a face expressive of power, almost as wilful as the nose, eyes and high cheekbones one finds in portraits of the great Duke of Wellington. It is a face, like Margaret Thatcher's, not of prettiness but command.' Hers is the countenance of a woman no longer prepared to be a victim but determined to fight for the survival of herself and her children. Shortly after her retirement from public life she made a promise to herself. 'I will be a puppet no longer. In the future I'm going to be true to my own beliefs and wishes,' she told friends who were impressed by the sturdiness of her convictions.

These days the princess will not allow her name—or photograph—to be taken in vain. Her vigorous pursuit through the courts of Bryce Taylor, the perpetrator of the Peeping-Tom photographs—in February 1995 she may be the first royal this century to appear as a witness in court—was matched by proposed actions against books, which she felt either besmirched her family name or breached a previous confidence. She was deeply unhappy when her former exercise trainer, Carol Ann Brown, blazoned her royal association over the cover of her latest video. While her actions betray her deep-seated insecurity and continual sense of feeling hunted, they also demonstrated a young woman no longer prepared to allow her friendship or name to be taken in vain. Again, when Captain James Hewitt phoned to explain why he had sold his story and subsequently appeared on television, she was astonished at his nerve. The conversation was short and sharp—and very one-sided.

Sometimes the paparazzi feel the full force of an aggressive, self-confident woman: 'Why don't you rape someone else?' she shouted at several cameramen during a private shopping trip, her extravagant language unwittingly echoing the philosophy of the so-called 'gender feminists' who believe that women are the victims of a male-dominated society. Cameramen quickly got used to seeing the sour expression, the averted head and the handbag strategically placed in front of her face. She complained to friends: 'They are trying to barge me now.' Soon she was dubbed 'the royal baglady' and described by royal-watchers as 'selectively mad'. They missed the point. It was her fervent wish to live as normal a life as possible and prove to the many doubting Thomases in the Metropolitan Police that she could survive without a permanent shadow. If that meant lying on the floor of a London taxi to avoid flashbulbs, sprinting out of fashionable restaurants and scowling at cameramen or, on one occasion, giving one persistent photographer the royal finger, so be it. As she told friends: 'I've gone beyond caring what the press think of me. It's what you think of yourself that counts.'

Her vigorous defence of her right to privacy coincided with a wider Palace assault on the curse of long-range photography, specifically outlawed in a new code of media conduct. One evening Prince Edward startled waiting photographers when he filmed them with a home-video camera outside the west London home of his girlfriend, Sophie Rhys-Jones. He wanted to use the film as evidence of press harassment.

On one occasion Diana approached a ground-floor apartment near her health centre at the Chelsea Harbour Club, which was a hideout for paparazzi. She thought she saw a movement and started shouting at the cameramen to go away. For once her instincts— it is her proud boast that she can smell a photographer from a hundred yards—were wrong. They were all hiding in a car nearby and watched in bewildered amusement as the Princess of Wales stood in her sports gear, yelling at a pair of curtains.

While the occasional confrontations with photographers made the headlines—and like other members of the Spencer family, she secretly enjoys a good shouting match—her new-found freedom soon paid pleasing dividends. When she was out shopping in Kensington she discovered that complete strangers, usually women, would approach her. They were diffident, apologetic but none the less eager to pour out their troubles to a woman they admired for her instinctive sympathy and inner strength. For the princess, so long isolated from the real world, it was a new experience and she happily lent an understanding ear as they talked about their problems. As she says: 'I like to live as normally as possible. Walking along the pavement without a bodyguard gives me such a thrill.' However, she would like to draw the line at tourists' requests for her autograph.

Simple pleasures please. An evening of ten-pin bowling with the young princes and friends in Berkshire was a quiet delight, even though she admits she wasn't much good. Undisturbed lunches with old chums are a joy. 'She was as sparky as a bird,' says one friend who thought her rather more sane than the newspaper editors who were branding her as off the rails. Others remarked on her solidity of purpose and serious commitment to the unpublicized substance of her life, her charity work.

The charity executives who lunch with her, the homeless, the AIDS sufferers and the battered women who talk to her, see a very different person from that depicted by the media. For many months now they have mixed with her privately and informally. They talk of the princess's generous spirit, her sense of humour and her genuine empathy with society's victims. 'Hers is not a show for public consumption,' remarked one charity administrator. Her guiding spirit is her grandmother, Cynthia Spencer, who the princess believes watches over her from the spirit world. Her grandmother had a reputation for quiet Christian charity, which Diana would like to emulate. Her interest in the metaphysical world comes from personal experience. As a teenager, for example, she sensed that her father, Earl Spencer, was about to be taken seriously ill on the day he had a brain haemorrhage. Since then she often senses that something is about to happen before it occurs, and she has spoken of her instinctive ability almost to 'see inside someone's soul' when she first meets them. Her psychic abilities and uncanny empathy with those making their last spiritual journey—'Death doesn't frighten me,' she says—strengthens her conviction that in another existence she was a nun. Perhaps that is why she so adores Mother Teresa of Calcutta. Her own sense of spirituality in the present, together with the sense of renewal and satisfaction that the act of giving, either emotionally or physically, brings have reinforced her genuine long-term commitment to helping those in need. It is therapeutic for Diana as well. She finds that she understands her own problems more clearly after discussions, for instance, with battered women, women suffering from post-natal depression or drug addicts. A common refrain is: 'She really seemed to understand me. It came from the heart.'

She moves easily into the role of ministering angel, especially as it puts her in control of the social situation. Her charismatic healing aura has uplifted many afflicted by chronic disease and encouraged those who nurse them. It takes a special kind of courage to be so intimately involved with the chronically sick. 'She has a wonderful understanding of people, a devotional love for those who are dying, which, given her youth, is quite extraordinary,' says a former nurse and regular visitor to Kensington Palace.

Examples abound. When friends recently asked her to visit a pensioner who was dying of a brain tumour she was pleased to help. Again, when her lady-in-waiting, Laura Lonsdale, lost her eleven-month-old son Louis through cot death syndrome, the princess spent many months counselling her through her grief. Her sensitivity and understanding were much appreciated by the family. 'The Princess of Wales is the nearest thing to an angel on earth,' said one relative. 'She has a unique quality of being able to comfort someone without being pushy or over the top. She has a magic touch all of her own.' A few weeks after the death of the British Labour Party leader, John Smith, she invited his widow and three daughters to Kensington Palace for a private lunch so that she could personally express her sympathy, and she took the time to write to the parents of baby Abbie Humphries who was kidnapped from hospital when just four hours old. As one of Diana's friends says: 'Her public image is one of beauty, grace and caring. Her private life is one of simplicity and humility. She has time for everyone, the old, the sick and the deprived.'

Her work is not a self-indulgence. The princess actively encourages her sons to join her on outings to give them a feel for the world beyond boarding school and palaces. It is especially important for William, as Diana argues: 'Through learning what I do and his father does he has got an insight in to what is coming his way. He's not hidden upstairs with the governess.' Her training has paid handsome dividends. Last winter she took him on a secret visit to the Passage day centre for the homeless in central London, accompanied by Cardinal Basil Hume. Her pride was evident as she introduced William to what many would consider the flotsam and jetsam of society. 'He loves it and that really rattles people,' she proudly told friends. Cardinal Hume was equally effusive. 'What an extraordinary child,' he told her. 'He has such dignity at such a young age.' That experience helped him to cope when a group of mentally handicapped children joined pupils from Ludgrove School for a Christmas party. Diana watched with delight as the future king gallantly helped these deprived youngsters join in the fun. 'I was so thrilled and proud. A lot of adults couldn't handle it,' she told friends. On another occasion, the princess received an appreciative letter from a mother of one of the boys in William's school dormitory. She wanted to express her thanks for William's kindness one night for looking after her son who had been taken ill.

It is a continuing education. During Ascot Week, a time of champagne, smoked salmon and fashionable frivolity for high society, the princess organized a special day out for her boys. It began quite normally. She took them for a spin in her new Audi convertible before treating them to an ice cream. While Diana indulged her boys, her private secretary, Patrick Jephson, was busy on the telephone, making the final arrangements with the nuns who run the Refuge night shelter for street people. At eight in the evening three cars, the first with the princess and her sons, the other two with the police bodyguards, pulled up outside the modest house in Westminster. The royal party was greeted by Sister Bridie Dowd and, while Diana mingled with the homeless men, William played chess with one of the men and Harry joined in a card game. Two hours later the boys were on their way back to Kensington Palace, a little older and a little wiser. The princess articulated her thinking about the upbringing of her boys in a speech on AIDS: 'I am only too aware of the temptation of avoiding harsh reality; not just for myself but for my own children too. Am I doing them a favour if I hide suffering and unpleasantness from them until the last possible minute? The last minutes which I choose for them may be too late. I can only face them with a choice based on what I know. The rest is up to them.'

While Prince Charles, immaculately dressed in a

top hat and tails paraded with high society at Ascot, the princess had another Ladies' Day in mind. This time she left the boys at home when she went to a hostel for homeless youngsters in a seedy part of London's Soho district. She chatted and joked with a group of young people, listening as they talked about their hopes, ambitions and favourite pop groups. After an hour she left the shelter, run by the Centrepoint charity, for a short drive to the so-called 'bullring', a cardboard city of waifs and strays, the hopeful and the hopeless nestling in the bowels of the London South Bank arts complex.

Her visit was low-key but politically loaded, coming just days after Prime Minister John Major had attacked beggars littering the streets and Prince Philip had argued that absolute poverty no longer existed in Britain. The princess was not there to pontificate but to learn, walking in the gloom beneath the arches led by a leather-clad woman and her mongrel dog. It was a curious scene. Normally when royalty mixes with society's victims there is an air of artifice about the whole proceedings; the place and the people are usually spruced up before a royal visit, while the smiling, elegantly dressed royal personage is surrounded by flunkeys and police as they meet a hand-picked cast of characters, of hospital patients, the old folk or the handicapped. Waiting in the wings is a flag-waving, flower-laden crowd. Royal events are contrived for the cameras, stage-managed for the royal programme and have all the spontaneity of a

Swiss railway timetable. They are by definition manufactured.

So the sight of the woman, who is still technically the future queen, unsmiling, unadorned and virtually unaccompanied, mixing with London's poorest, confounded critics. The scene intrigues precisely because it reveals Diana behaving like an ordinary person, rather than an actress in a contrived drama. As the Princess of Wales crunched over broken glass, the smell of stale booze all pervasive, she was met with the sight of bearded figures dressed in rags and tatters, like some primitive tribe, slowly emerging from their cavelike box dwellings. As she chatted, teenage boys played on their skateboards nearby, and elsewhere drunks slumped against the dreary concrete pillars, a mess of newspapers and bottles at their feet. She asked about their diet, their lifestyle and commended one cardboard-city veteran for managing to manhandle a real bed into his flimsy home. When another vagrant emerged half-naked before her, he excused his appearance by joking that his Savile Row suit was at the cleaners. There was much resentment among them bubbling beneath the surface. One long-term inhabitant, known as Herman the German, his beard almost at waist length, spoke fiercely of his anger at the official attacks on beggars. Others condemned John Major and her father-in-law, Prince Philip. Some thanked her for listening to their case. It was a high-risk, unpredictable and potentially dangerous encounter between the princess and a forgotten, sullen and embittered people.

Other private visits have not been so physically fraught, but they underline her commitment to forging a new life that gives her personal fulfilment and yet contributes to the well-being of the handful of charities she now supports. In the last year she has counselled distressed and battered women at the charity shelter, Refuge, comforted AIDS patients at the Mildmay Mission in east London and visited drug addicts at hostels in central London. In November 1994, for example, she visited Broadmoor Prison in Berkshire on a private visit in order to obtain an insight in to the workings of a high-security prison. 'Living with the royal family is an ideal preparation for going to Broadmoor,' she joked with a friend afterwards. Like the visit to the 'bullring', there is no fuss, no frills and no formality, in vivid contrast to her only official charity engagement this year, when she visited the Great Ormond Street children's hospital in February.

The smiles, the flowers, the flashbulbs and the dated fashions seemed like a throwback to a different era. She too felt it was a rather tired affair and the experience reinforced the wisdom of her decision to re-evaluate her public life. None the less columnist Peter McKay's comments still hurt her. 'She was like a cranked-out, old seaside comic who, having decided she was being typecast, takes herself off into the wilderness to rethink her act, only to turn up again, worse than ever.'

The princess, emotionally battered and bruised, had already taken the point the previous year. Her strategic retreat from royal duties last December gave her the opportunity to develop her own blueprint: to use her personality and position in a way which was effective, and to avoid the hullabaloo of traditional royal visits. The difficult issue to be resolved is that, in her position as a working princess, she provided the opportunity for the charities to raise thousands of pounds, as well as promoting issues to the front pages. Her private visits have given her the chance to perform meaningful and satisfying work, but they do not provide a wider resonance, those ripples of public awareness that are only created when the full panoply of royalty is employed. It is a Catch-22 situation, with no easy solution.

Over the last few years her shredder at Kensington Palace has swallowed dozens of memos, documents and plans detailing numerous schemes to revitalize and refocus her public persona. The idea of a Princess of Wales trust or foundation, which would act as an umbrella organization to reflect Diana's interests, and channel the torrent of requests she receives, has long been on the agenda, but it has never got off the ground because of objections from Prince Charles who believed, probably correctly, that it would take the shine from his own highly successful Prince's Trust.

During a Mediterranean cruise one summer, Diana had the opportunity to discuss the idea with Greek billionaire, John Latsis. The topic arose during a light-hearted conversation about the origin of his vast fortune. 'I broke people's legs,' he joked. On a more serious note he felt that the princess's international status and popularity would make the establishment of her own trust a cast-iron success. It is a concept which has appealed to the princess precisely because it would give her control of policy and strategy, as well as giving her the latitude to work privately at the cutting edge of charity work. She also welcomed the chance to shed the image of decorative figurehead or smiling 'Lady Bountiful'.

In May 1993, flesh was put on the bare bones of these plans during a series of meetings between the film director, David Puttnam, her private secretary, Patrick Jephson, and Les Rudd of the National AIDS Trust. They discussed ways of using film premieres more sparingly and productively. The princess had made clear that she wanted to do less 'flashbulb' charity appearances and more hands-on work. Conversely, she recognized that these glittering events were an easy way for her charities to raise money.

It was a start but not a solution. During the autumn of 1993, a grander vision was contemplated, this time with an international dimension. It would concentrate on disadvantaged women and children, particularly those with AIDS. Lord Palumbo, who pays for Diana's lawyer, Lord Mishcon, and Lord Rothschild, who funded the restoration of Spencer House, were earmarked as potential backers. This time, however, the princess was the stumbling block, her profound disillusion with public life leading her to the conclusion that a significant sabbatical was needed to recharge her batteries. However, an international approach still appealed, not least because it neatly sidestepped Charles's complaints that she was hogging the limelight. As Diana and the rest of the royal family knew only too well, 1994 was his year, a time to celebrate the twenty-fifth anniversary of his investiture as Prince of Wales. Courtiers worked long and hard to ensure that there were few clouds to overshadow his days of glory. As Diana remarked to friends: 'His office are paranoid to make sure that everything goes smoothly. They are terrified of it going wrong for their boss.' All the royals were affected. The Duchess of York told the princess that she was under intense pressure to delay divorcing Prince Andrew, as she was legally entitled to do in March 1994, while Prince Edward informed his girlfriend, Sophie Rhys-Jones, that a wedding was off the agenda for the time being.

For Diana the thought of leaving the domestic stage for an international forum was seductive. Her appeal to Prime Minister John Major to be given the wider brief of a roaming ambassador and so leave the domestic stage for Prince Charles had reached other ears. The British Red Cross had been building gradually their links with the princess. Chief executive, Mike Whitlam, had tuned into her desire for an executive, hands-on approach to her work, and suggested she attend a training course with senior managers in America. A casual conversation about her hobbies—she complained that as she was followed to the cinema by cameramen she had taken up gocarting, a sport which also gives her a satisfying sense of control—lead to a suggestion to take part in a go-carting fundraising event. Significantly it took place just hours before her 'time and space' speech and one of the last people to wish her well was Mike Whitlam. In the weeks before she retired she was quietly made vice-president of the British Red Cross, a sign of the direction she was about to take. (Indeed, the new job bore out her astrologer's assertion that a 'golden opportunity' would land in her lap at the end of 1993.) She was initially apprehensive, worried that the organization might just use her for PR and concerned that its image was too set in its ways. 'The Red Cross is no good for me because it is too old an institution. Women and children's health around the world would interest me more,' she remarked to friends. Her fears were balanced by the prospect of getting her teeth into the job of roving emissary for an internationally respected organization. 'I've got it all, it's a huge job,' she said enthusiastically.

Around this hub, other charities gravitated as they jostled for Diana's time and interest. Her private secretary, Patrick Jephson, who had been tempted to work full-time for the Red Cross but was persuaded to stay by Diana's side, was pivotal, knitting together her charitable involvement and sifting through the plethora of proposals and requests. The Mildmay Mission, for example, played the international card, discussing the possibility of the princess laying the foundation stone for two new hospitals in Tanzania and Uganda, combining this with a tour of the AIDS front-line in Africa. One of her Army regiments invited her to select youngsters for a course they were sponsoring in

Kenya, while the Red Cross, through the good offices of Lord Archer, lobbied for her presence on the first passenger train through the Channel Tunnel scheduled for June 1994, although the excursion, in aid of charity, hit the buffers because of delays in opening the project. However, as Diana's private secretary frequently pointed out to the charity lobbyists, there was no magic wand that would entice the princess back into the limelight. Proposed comeback dates were fixed optimistically for February, then September, until finally charities accepted that they could not start pencilling her in for work until 1995 at the earliest.

Diana's search for a new style to make the most of her substance was never going to be an overnight process, although there was a dawning public awareness that the Red Cross was to be her chosen path. When she was appointed to a special advisory commission of the International Red Cross, the place of the organization in the princess's thinking seemed to be assured. Inevitably, and perhaps not inaccurately, comparisons were made with the way Princess Anne grew in international standing and stature thanks to her successful association with The Save the Children Fund. Diana's visits to Geneva to discuss the plight of the world's refugees, particularly the horrific tragedy in Rwanda, were suitably low-key. For once she was just a face in the crowd, especially on her second trip in July when she and Patrick Jephson stayed at the Inter-Continental hotel. As luck would have it, the hotel was the venue for the Bosnian peace talks and the dozens of film crews were more interested in chatting to peace envoys like Lord Owen and America's Secretary of State, Warren Christopher, than the princess. She was able to sit unnoticed in the lounge and watch the World Cup match between Brazil and America. 'My boys are football mad, so I've got to be up to speed with the results. The trouble is I am always put in goal,' she explained.

As her modest team settled into this new rhythm of royal work, remnants of her previous life began to fall away. Only days after her retirement speech she visited St James's Palace to reassure her secretarial staff that their jobs were safe and asked them to give her time to recast her priorities. They were not entirely confident and several clerks soon found more secure employment elsewhere. The princess herself signalled the change in her life a few weeks later when she held a tea party for a handful of girlfriends at Kensington Palace, where she gave them the pick from her official working clothes. There would be no going back, a sentiment underlined in May this year by Patrick Jephson at the farewell party of her equerry, Captain Edward Musto, who was returning to the Royal Marines. Jephson told the throng of charity workers and palace staff assembled in the Billiard Room at Buckingham Palace that Musto's departure marked the end of an era.

The peeling away of the layers of protocol surrounding the princess meant that she was far more involved in the day-to-day running of her life than ever before. Just as her charities were thinking carefully how they could dovetail their work around her ambitions, so she began to use her network of contacts to try and help them. She and Jephson acted as discreet lobbyists for selected charities, approaching movers and shakers in industry, the arts, media and government for assistance. There were frequent working lunches at Kensington Palace to set the seal on various schemes. She personally organized a Vogue cover portrait to celebrate her thirty-third birthday to raise thousands of pounds for two of her charities, the Chicken Shed Theatre group and DEBRA, which funds research into a rare children's illness. This photograph inevitably made headlines and produced more accusations that she was once again moving into the limelight. In fact it was merely a public manifestation of the quiet activity taking place behind the closed doors of Kensington Palace.

As she struggled slowly to make sense of her life, she realized that there were many enemies waiting outside the palace gates, eager to see her fall flat on her face. Doors which had been wide open now were slammed shut. When she asked if Princes William and Harry could visit Lippets Hill, the police weapons' training centre in Essex, Metropolitan Police chiefs, still smarting from her decision to live unprotected, coolly informed her that she would have to go through 'official channels'. They made it clear that 'the boys have a father as well', implying that he should be consulted before the police became involved. Furthermore, senior officers made it clear that any request for occasional protection at public events would have to be made in writing. There was resentment too from her bodyguards when the princess asked them to stop photographers filming her on her balcony in Lech, as she had only reluctantly agreed to their presence at the last minute. During that holiday she sent out confusing signals to all concerned. One moment she was happily skiing with journalists, the next she was bursting into tears in front of cameramen and pleading with them to leave her alone. For once, the paparazzi and her press officer, Geoff Crawford, were united in bafflement.

While Diana has been universally described as manipulative, there is a rich seam of naivety and amateurism in her guile. She will ski with the reporters she knows, expect to be left alone by photographers and then complain to her press officer because he has failed to prevent the paparazzi from hounding her. She is skilful in face-to-face encounters with those with influence, like politicians or editors, but breathtakingly incapable of understanding the long-term consequences of some of her actions. Strategy is not her strong suit. As she told chess player, Nigel Short: 'We end up in these public positions but we are never prepared for the publicity and how to deal with it.' Suspicious and critical of the way the Palace handled her press relations, the princess, again wanting to take charge of her life, decided to handle them herself. At first she was successful. When agents acting on behalf of the American TV personality, Oprah Winfrey, contacted the princess's office about the possibility of an interview, Diana decided to give them a hearing. The prospect of a multimillion-dollar donation to her charities was tempting, but after meeting Oprah for lunch she decided that the show's format was not for her. Again, the Australian wit and television pundit, Clive James, an old friend of Charles and Diana's, was another big-name star pitching for the princess. They discussed his plans over lunch on several occasions and Diana was so impressed that she secretly went to see one of his shows. He was put high on the list if she ever did decide to give a television interview. Diana made it clear that she, not Buckingham Palace, would be the final arbiter. Again, she used her friendship with Lady Stevens, the wife of the chief executive of Express Newspapers, Lord Stevens, to arrange meetings with Nick Lloyd and Eve Pollard, the husband-and-wife team who then edited, respectively, London's *Daily Express* and *Sunday Express*. The princess was concerned at the constant barrage of sniping stories in the *Sunday Express* and convinced Pollard to call off the editorial bloodhounds. It worked for a time.

However, it was the *Express*'s chief rival, the *Daily Mail*, which received the editorial fruits of her largesse. For many months the princess and her associates used the newspaper to drip-feed a series of pleasant, 'good-news' stories about her life and works: details, for instance, of her holiday in Florida, and how she had played the Good Samaritan by helping an elderly couple whose car had overheated in heavy London traffic as she returned home from lunch with

William and Harry. At first these disclosures concerned her bodyguards, then the rest of Fleet Street and inevitably the Buckingham Palace press office, who in turn informed more senior courtiers, including Sir Robert Fellowes. Their worries that the princess was flirting with danger by her close association with a tabloid newspaper were finally conveyed to the Queen. Even though she was warned by the police against fraternizing with tabloid journalists, her contacts continued.

It was an accident waiting to happen and it all started with a simple weekend break at a tennis ranch in Spain. For the princess, it was to be another step on the long road to a private life, a world without bodyguards, prying officials or long-lens cameras. It all went disastrously wrong from the moment Diana and her friends, Kate Menzies and Catherine Soames, boarded the British Airways flight. Thoughts of a private vacation were jettisoned when they spotted a Sky television crew who were on their way to interview bank robbery suspect, Ronnie Knight. At Malaga Airport a gaggle of photographers was waiting, not for them, but the errant Knight. When they spotted Diana, the hunt was on.

Like a trio of teenage schoolgirls allowed out of boarding school for the first time, there was a juvenile naivety about their progress. For once there were no baggage masters, bodyguards or equerries to smooth the way. They hunted for their own luggage trolleys and then, realizing they had not booked a car for their onward journey, queued with other tourists for a taxi

to take them to the tennis complex r
Wimbledon champion, Lew Hoad. These
abroad arrived hot and dishevelled, and w
impressed by the accommodation. As they pond
their next move they bumped into hair stylist, George
Guy, who offered to take them to the nearby Byblos
Andaluz, a luxurious complex, complete with golf
courses, tennis courts and swimming pools. They
piled into his modest Ford Escort car and arranged
that he should take them back to the airport for their
return journey.

Their private calamity turned into a public catas-
trophe when Spanish photographers, who pestered
the girls at their hotel and jostled Diana at the airport,
claimed to have snapped the princess sunbathing
topless. They wanted a million pounds for the shots.
The issue of whether or not she sunbathed topless—
the princess vigorously denied the charge and the
pictures were bought by the proprietor of Hello!
magazine to stop them being printed—was quickly
overshadowed by her behaviour once back in Britain.
An hour-long private meeting between Diana and
Daily Mail reporter, Richard Kay, in her Audi sports
car that was parked behind Harrods, was photographed. In Kay's report the following day, he talked
of Diana's feelings of 'utter humiliation' at the alleged
topless pictures. It was 'like a rape' the princess was
reported to have told a friend. That friend, exposed
under the Sun headline 'Two-Faced Diana', was none
other than Kay himself.

If the topless pictures saga was embarrassing, this

atest episode saw her stock inside Buckingham Palace go into freefall. Before the *Sun* story was published, the princess decided to eat humble pie and apologize personally to her husband. After the meeting she was left in no doubt that he was unhappy about her collusion with the press and the manner in which it had been revealed. His staff weren't. She remarked later that they could scarcely suppress their glee. One of Charles's aides observed: 'She is not taking any sensible advice. Her approach is very short-term.' Others were scathingly dismissive. As one of the prince's supporters said: 'His side are fed up with her. They think that she is a nuisance and while there was a campaign against her there isn't now because she scores enough own goals herself.' A few days later, her boys put the episode into perspective. 'Did you really go topless in Spain?' they asked incredulously. 'No, I certainly didn't,' she replied. There was an audible sigh of relief from her children. 'Thank goodness for that, mummy,' they cheekily replied, 'because you haven't got much to show anyway.'

It should have been a salutary lesson, and for a few days the princess was suitably chastened. Still, her determination to handle her own media image continued, with devastating results. Perhaps the most damaging incident of her royal career—even the normally restrained BBC called her behaviour 'bizarre'—concerned allegations that she had made nuisance phone calls to her friends, Oliver and Diane Hoare, at their Chelsea home. The couple, who have known both the prince and princess for many years, had featured high on the paparazzi hit-list for many months. They knew that the princess had been seen frequently with the urbane old Etonian and so photographers regularly prowled past Hoare's £2 million home and Belgravia art gallery. In March 1994, when he escorted the princess home while his wife was in Marrakesh, Morocco, he took the unusual step of telephoning Prince Charles to reassure him that their friendship was entirely proper. 'I've known both the Prince and Princess of Wales for many years—they are friends and I get on well with them both,' he told enquirers.

It was a series of nuisance telephone calls several months earlier which brought unwanted front-page attention for the diffident Hoare. For many weeks, the Hoare residence had been plagued by unnerving phone calls. The phone would ring and after it was answered the caller would remain silent. At times there would be up to twenty calls a week, and on one occasion three came within the space of nine minutes. However, in October 1993, Diane Hoare received an abusive phone call, and this prompted her to call in the police. The police contacted British Telecom Nuisance Calls Bureau who traced the calls to three venues: Diana's private apartments at Kensington Palace, her sister Lady Sarah McCorquodale's home and public telephone boxes near to Kensington Palace, and also Diana's private mobile phone.

Details of the top-secret investigation were leaked to a Sunday newspaper, *News of the World*, which printed its scoop on 21 August 1994 under the headline: 'Di's cranky phone calls to married tycoon'. The implication was clear—the Princess of Wales was the silent caller who had so disturbed the Hoare household. While the story seemed sensational, in common with most tabloid revelations it would have been forgotten within a few days if the princess had not set in train a series of events which further damaged her image.

On the Saturday morning before publication, the *News of the World* twice contacted Hoare informing him that they were running the story about the nuisance calls. Just ten minutes after the second call, *News of the World* royal editor, Clive Goodman, was amazed to be contacted by tabloid rival, Richard Kay. Astonishingly, Kay said that he was not acting as a tabloid journalist but as a 'friend of the Princess of Wales', and went on to explain these calls in an off-the-record briefing. He claimed, rather preposterously, that a member of Diana's much-reduced staff had made the calls, because Hoare, who was a self-appointed intermediary between the prince and princess, had 'at times reduced Diana to tears'. Then the tabloid journalist added: 'She has some very loyal, and perhaps misguided people working for her and they took the matter into their own hands.'

While Kay was giving this version of events, the princess tried in vain to contact her lawyer, Lord Mishcon. Just a few hours after Kay spoke to the *News of the World*, the princess and Kay arranged a secret rendezvous in a quiet square in west London. They spent nearly three hours together in his car discussing the implications of the story. Unfortunately for Diana, cameraman Glenn Harvey, who snapped the couple together following her Spanish débâcle, was once more on the spot, photographing them deep in conversation. Normally, when Kay was acting as Diana's unofficial press officer, he would pass off her comments as coming from a 'close friend', thus distancing the princess from the remarks. Realizing that photographs of them together would be plastered all over Monday's tabloids, executives at the *Daily Mail* decided there was no point in continuing the charade. The story appeared as a 'world exclusive' interview with Diana, under the headline: 'What have I done to deserve this?' While the story provided an enormous coup for Kay and the *Daily Mail*, for Diana it provided a huge headache.

In her unprecedented interview the princess asked plaintively: 'What have I done to deserve this? I feel I am being destroyed. There is absolutely no truth in it. Do you realize that whoever is trying to destroy me is inevitably damaging the institution of monarchy as well? Somewhere someone is going to make out that I am mad, that I am guilty by association, that the mud will stick. I know everyone wants me to be having affairs and this man fits, but it's not true.'

Her comments were met by calls for an investigation into the police by Members of Parliament and a large degree of cynicism by the public. One newspaper commented acidly: 'High level conspiracy against the royal family—or one woman's descent into madness?' More importantly, Scotland Yard, Buckingham Palace and Mr Hoare did not issue any denial of the *News of the World*'s claim that Diana was the phone pest. Diana subsequently criticized Oliver Hoare for not supporting her, telling friends that she thought he was 'acting like a scared rabbit'.

For his part, Kay changed his version of events in the few hours that passed between his phone call to the *News of the World*, blaming a member of Diana's staff, and the printing of his exclusive interview. In the *Daily Mail* story he said: 'Unresolved, though, was the one central question: could they [the calls] have been made by someone else? There has been a claim that a member of the princess's staff had been quizzed, although the details are far from clear.' In fact, the claim had been made by Kay himself. However, he conceded, presumably with Diana's approval, that she had telephoned Hoare at the time the tapping was being carried out. He added tellingly: 'It is possible that she would have replaced the receiver if his wife answered—perhaps unwittingly triggering the family's fears that they were receiving nuisance calls.'

If Diana were the mystery caller, it would not have come as a complete surprise to her circle of friends, and especially, according to comments Kay made in the *News of the World*, that she blamed Oliver Hoare and her staff. If it were true, it would be indicative of her inability to accept responsibility for her actions, and a willingness to censure everybody except herself. For many years the princess has been something of a phone junkie, spending countless hours chatting to her friends and advisers. It is a measure of her isolation inside Kensington Palace that the phone has been her best friend.

Over the years, Diana has always had one or two advisers to whom she turns, sometimes telephoning as often as twenty times a day. The recipients of these calls are nearly always older married men who can provide mature advice and counsel. As one long-term friend admitted: 'She is more demanding than any wife would ever be. She often calls when she is in distress and wants a sympathetic audience. It is certainly the case that on many occasions Diana has put the phone down when my wife answered. Naturally my wife felt very angry and sometimes alarmed but we both understand the problem—Diana doesn't want to seem to be a nuisance for taking up my time. It's also important to realize that she telephones at times of distress, often in tears, and she only wants to speak to one person. She would understandably feel embarrassed talking to someone who was not so close to her. Everyone is aware of the loneliness of her position so we make allowances.'

Nevertheless, wives of Diana's confidants do feel resentful, not only because she takes up their husbands' time, but also because the calls are emotionally draining. One friend describes her phone style: 'What I call the "Poor me" tone is the most common type of call. Sometimes you feel as if you've run a marathon afterwards. It's very tiring.'

Sadly her attempt at 'do-it-yourself' media relations

had once again proved disastrous. While it was embarrassing that the Hoare phone story was made public, the major problems were encountered, as former American president Richard Nixon found in the Watergate affair, in the attempt to cover up the scandal. These efforts highlighted once more her crippling isolation from the royal family, her naivety and her obsession with the tabloid press. It was an affair which also exposed a Spencer characteristic—the naive, yet reckless, tempting of fate and authority.

Tumbles were inevitable as the princess groped her way from the chill royal peaks towards friendlier climes. Occasionally, this intrepid social mountaineer used the existing guide ropes of royalty to give her a helping hand. On her way to Heathrow Airport for a Red Cross meeting in Geneva, for example, she allowed her chauffeur, Steve Davies, to use the police blue light she carried to help her cut through heavy traffic. It earned him an official reprimand. Another time, two police constables were ticked off after they left a note on Diana's windscreen falsely stating that her car had broken down, which had enabled her to leave it on a yellow line while she kept a lunch date at San Lorenzo in Knightsbridge. Just as her privileges had exacted a high price in personal freedom, so she was learning to pay for her new liberties in the hard currency of her royal entitlements.

Diana's problem was that she had left one world without a clear idea of where she was going. The public and media were impatient for her either to return to the fold, forge a defined new life or fall from grace. They were uneasy and intolerant of this hiatus as she sincerely endeavoured quietly to carve a new lifestyle. Everything from her fashions—she was accused of looking like a suburban housewife by *Tatler* magazine—to her battles with photographers, came under hostile scrutiny. It was the unfairness that hurt her most. Accustomed to an adoring press, she was startled by how quickly reverence and respect had evaporated since discarding the invisible but protective cloak of royalty.

She watched with growing concern as her husband's star gradually grew brighter. His was a much easier task. Unlike the princess, Prince Charles was not rocking the boat, merely waiting his turn to be captain of the good ship Windsor. With the voluble support of the Prime Minister, the Cabinet, the Church, the rest of the royal family, Establishment newspapers and the Great and the Good together with a professional office staff, he was by definition able to play the waiting game. As his private secretary, Richard Aylard, remarked: 'There is no point going for some quick popularity fix. As the future king, the Prince of Wales is in a long-term business.'

The centrepiece of the Prince of Wales's long haul back to credibility following the collapse of his marriage and the Camillagate affair was a documentary by the television broadcaster Jonathan Dimbleby to mark the twenty-fifth anniversary of his investiture as Prince of Wales. From the moment the prince informed Diana of the project, in the summer of 1992, Diana was on tenterhooks. She carefully monitored progress of the filming, concerned that her role as a mother would be questioned and worried that her estranged husband might use their children as innocent props in what she imagined was to be a pro-Charles propaganda exercise. Her conversations with friends were peppered with references to the Dimbleby project, as she wondered aloud if it would burnish or tarnish Charles's image in the public's mind. Her consternation intensified when publicity material for the companion book trumpeted the claim that it was 'the complete riposte' to *Diana, Her True Story* which was sympathetic to her and which many believe was written with her tacit approval.

One of Diana's rare appearances in the two-and-a-half-hour show came when she was filmed in the winter of 1993 at a concert in remembrance of her grandmother, Ruth, Lady Fermoy, which was held at Buckingham Palace. In a poignant sequence dealing with the collapse of the marriage, it showed a stern-faced princess, seated next to Prince Philip, looking straight ahead as the musicians played a melancholy air from Bach's concerto for two violins. Meanwhile, the prince, sitting apart from the princess with the Queen and Queen Mother, was shown wistfully gazing into the middle distance, while a tear gently rolled down his cheek. The scene served its purpose, showing a shrewish princess and a sensitive prince. Television presenter, Anne Diamond, watched the poignant scene and complained: 'Dimbleby's cynical attempt to have us believe that Charles was actually in tears over it was incredible . . . If he was moved, it was because

Above: Diana, Princes William and Harry and friends Catherine Soames and Kate Menzies are all smiles as they set off for a horse-drawn sleigh ride during their skiing holiday in Lech, Austria. The boys are proving to be adventurous and competitive skiers, trying to outdo one another in daring ski 'jumps' (Dave Chancellor/Alpha)

Below: The princess and her elder son at the 1994 Wimbledon Ladies' Final, where they saw Spain's Conchita Martinez beat nine-times winner Martina Navratilova. Diana has played socially with Martina and another Wimbledon winner, Steffi Graf (Dave Chancellor/Alpha)

The Princess of Wales and Prince Harry walk back to Sandringham House after the traditional church service on Christmas Day. Although Diana only stayed with the royal family for twenty-four hours, *Prince Charles was concerned that her presence would give the public the impression that they were trying to effect a reconciliation* (Dave Chancellor/Alpha)

Right: A weekend ritual, which Prince Harry always looks forward to, is the visit to the local sweetshop, a couple of hundred yards away from his Ludgrove boarding school in Berkshire
(All Action)

Below: The princess and the overfamiliar Virgin Airlines' tycoon, Richard Branson, at Gatwick Airport for the unveiling of his new Airbus. It was one of Diana's last engagements before her withdrawal from royal duties
(Russell Cisby/Nunn Syndication)

The appointment of Alexandra 'Tiggy' Legge-Bourke by Prince Charles to act as companion for Princes William and Harry has annoyed and upset the princess, who believes that Tiggy is taking on the role of surrogate mother. It is easy to see why. She is of the same generation and social class as the princess and mixes easily with Charles's circle. If Diana had hired a man to act as proxy father there would have been uproar, but Tiggy's position has excited little comment—except from the princess. On their arrival at Zurich Airport for a skiing trip in Klosters (*right*), they look for all the world like a happy family. In the bus Tiggy makes sure that Harry's seat belt is properly fastened (*above*), and in the village of Tetbury, near Charles's Highgrove home, she leads the boys safely across the road after buying them an ice cream (*below*) (Nunn Syndication; Dave Parker/Alpha; Joan Wakeham/Alpha)

Right: The princess, followed by Princess Margaret, leaves the royal yacht *Britannia* for celebrations in Portsmouth to commemorate the 50th anniversary of D-Day. Since her withdrawal from public life, the princess has agreed to maintain her links with the Armed Services (Dave Chancellor/Alpha)

Below: A doorman at the Ritz Hotel stands with the princess as she waits for her car after leaving a party to celebrate the election of Sir James Goldsmith as a Euro MP. Her hostile gaze at the camera was analysed by at least one psychiatrist as signifying her 'inner turmoil' (Miguel/Alpha)

On the evening that the Prince of Wales confessed his adultery on prime-time television, the princess, escorted by Lord Palumbo, was the guest of honour at a gala banquet at the Serpentine Gallery, of which she is patron
(Dave Chancellor/Alpha)

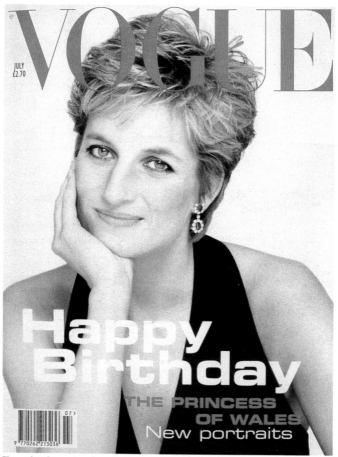

VOGUE

JULY
£2.70

Happy
Birthday

THE PRINCESS
OF WALES
New portraits

French photographer Patrick Dermarchelier was
commissioned by the princess to take a series of portraits for
her thirty-third birthday. All proceeds from *Vogue*'s
publication of the pictures went to charity

Above: The princess takes her sons for a spin in her Audi convertible. However, it is not all fun and frivolity. Later that evening Diana and the boys secretly visited a homeless centre for down-and-out men. It is part of William's training as the future king (Glenn Harvey)

Below: The princess and her companion, art dealer Oliver Hoare, return to Kensington Palace after dining with friends at a Chinese restaurant. Hoare, who is married with two children, took the unusual step of telephoning Prince Charles to assure him of the propriety of their relationship (Glenn Harvey)

Above: Diana with the Queen Mother and the Duke of Edinburgh, two members of the royal family who vigorously expressed their disapproval of Diana's behaviour prior to the separation. Since then there has been a thaw between the duke and the princess. He congratulated Diana after she initiated legal action against a newspaper group for publishing 'Peeping-Tom' pictures of her in a gym
(Richard Gillard/Camera Press)

Above: The princess at a D-Day ceremony for the unveiling of a memorial to the Canadian forces who took part in both World Wars (Photographers International)

Left: In May 1994 the princess attended her first meeting of a new advisory commission of the International Red Cross. At the seminar, held in Geneva, the princess was pictured discussing the agenda with chairman Darell Jones. The relief agency is one of only a handful of charities Diana has maintained links with since her withdrawal from public life (Tim Graham)

Left: A weekend break in Spain turned sour for the princess and her friends, when paparazzi claimed they had pictured her bathing topless. She escaped from their attentions thanks to help from hairdresser George Guy, who turned royal chauffeur for the day (Rafael Guervos/All Action)

Below: The princess, Princess Michael of Kent and her teenage son, Lord Frederick Windsor, at the 1994 Wimbledon Men's Final, which saw American Pete Sampras retain his title in an easy victory over Goran Ivanisevic. Diana's royal next-door neighbour has been a stalwart supporter during a difficult year (Tim Rooke/Rex Features)

The princess and Prince Harry watch the action at the 1994 British Grand Prix at Silverstone. A keen race fan, Prince Harry was thrilled when he was allowed to sit behind the wheel of a Formula Three car under the watchful eye of former champion Jackie Stewart

(S. Jackson/All Action)

Above: The princess enjoys a day-out at the Thorpe Park leisure centre, with her boys and many of her Kensington Palace staff, including her chauffeur, butler, dresser and their children (Nunn Syndication)

Right: The princess and Prince Edward's girlfriend, Sophie Rhys-Jones, at the wedding of Princess Margaret's daughter, Lady Sarah Armstrong-Jones, to Daniel Chatto. Diana was criticized by Prince Charles for attending the public rather than the private side of the occasion; she went to the church service but missed the reception at Clarence House, the Queen Mother's home (All Action)

Diana looks almost as excited as Damon Hill, the 1994 winner of the British Grand Prix, when she presents him with the trophy. The unassuming Englishman was all the more delighted with his victory as his father, the legendary Graham Hill, never achieved a win at Silverstone
(Ross Parry/Rex Features)

of the music. I doubt if he's shed any tears for Diana.' Long before the film was broadcast the princess had complained about the event. Her suspicions had been raised earlier by an unusual phone call from the Prince of Wales a few days before the concert asking if the boys could go along as well. She could not understand why he was so keen to have William and Harry present but when she arrived and saw the film crew she realized the underlying purpose. While he greeted the princess with a kiss she complained afterwards that she and her family had been ill-served throughout the evening. 'He treated me badly,' she told a friend, which goes some way to explaining her unhappy expression.

In an attempt to placate her fears about the documentary, a lunch between the princess and Jonathan Dimbleby was arranged at the west London home of a mutual friend. During that meeting, in April 1994, he asked her for an interview—which she declined—before reassuring her that her role as a mother would not be denigrated. Then they discussed various aspects of the royal marriage up to the period in 1987 when Prince Charles trekked into the Kalahari desert with Sir Laurens van der Post. Dimbleby made it clear too that she would have a modest role in the companion book to accompany the documentary. The meeting did not have the desired effect. Diana felt unsettled and wary, especially when he pursued a line of questioning about the divorce, which echoed that of her husband. As the publicity hype built to a crescendo, the princess plaintively asked a friend:

'How on earth am I going to get through this week?' It coincided with a further swing in the pendulum of media sentiment about the princess, moving away from adoration to abuse. A few nights before the screening of the programme, scheduled for late June, she attended a party at the Ritz Hotel to celebrate the birthday of her friend, Annabel Goldsmith, and the election of her husband, Sir James Goldsmith, as a Euro MP. It coincided with the release of pre-publicity photographs of the Charles documentary by Central TV, an event over which she had no control. As she was leaving the party, she deliberately stood with her head bowed to prevent the paparazzi getting a clear shot, a further example of her policy towards photographers. Yet, depending on the tabloid you read, the princess, described as 'sly and scheming', was either wilfully courting the limelight in an attempt to overshadow Charles or revealing an 'inner turmoil that she can no longer hide.' Her anxieties were fuelled when one tabloid editor warned her staff that unless she made a comeback they would declare open war on her.

In her increasingly isolated and vulnerable position, she prudently decided against taking the opportunity to watch an advance viewing of the film. While 13 million people settled down to see the show, the princess decided to go out and enjoy herself. She had a long-standing engagement to attend a dinner at the Serpentine Gallery of which she is patron. Even here there were hiccups. She was irritated when the couturiers Valentino prematurely announced that she would be wearing one of their dresses for the function. Once again, determined to make the point that she was in charge of her life, she left it in the wardrobe and donned a flirty little number by Christina Stambolian. She could not have made a more appropriate choice, its style shouting the message: 'Whatever Charles may do, I'm having a ball.'

She was among friends, chatting amiably with Peter Palumbo and his wife Hayat, Lord Gowrie, gallery director, Julia Peyton-Jones, and assorted artists, writers and actors, including Jeremy Irons and Joan Collins. It was a high-octane, sophisticated international event, more in keeping with cosmopolitan California than central London. The following day she read the screaming headlines about Charles's confession of adultery, but restricted herself to the comment that she did not think television to be an appropriate medium for the future king to be discussing such a personal matter. It was a view shared by many inside the Palace who were uneasy about such public soul-searching.

Ironically, much of the programme was a reworking of Sir Alastair Burnet's 1985 fly-on-the-wall documentary about the prince and princess. Like Burnet, Dimbleby focused on the background to the prince's working life: his private meetings, overseas visits and public engagements. Where it differed was in featuring Charles's controversial views on the Church—he wanted to be the 'Defender of Faith' rather than 'Defender of the Faith'—and his anguished confirmation that he had been unfaithful to the Princess of

Wales. In response to the question, 'Were you, did you try to be faithful and honourable to your wife when you took on the vow of marriage?' the prince replied: 'Yes absolutely.' Dimbleby continued, 'And were you?' The prince said, 'Yes', but after a brief pause, 'until it became irretrievably broken down, us both having tried.' Asked about his relationship with Camilla Parker Bowles he confirmed that she will continue to be the mainstay of his life in spite of her perceived role in the marriage break-up. He described her as 'a great friend of mine . . . she has been a friend for a very long time and will continue to be a friend for a very long time.' Before the interview, Charles spent many hours in conversation with Camilla Parker Bowles. In a further intervention the next day, Dimbleby made it clear that, in off-camera conversations with the prince, he understood that the marriage had broken down 'any time after 1986' just five years after the wedding at St Paul's Cathedral.

Less clear was the question of divorce. In his TV interview the prince was evasive, saying that it was 'very much in the future' and 'not a consideration in my mind', adding that it was a matter between himself and the princess. Certainly his public admission of adultery, that in effect he was to blame, broke the psychological and legal stalemate surrounding discussions about their divorce and the financial settlement. From the beginning Diana was adamant that she would not be the one to initiate divorce proceedings. That decision had to come from Prince Charles. It created an impasse which lasted for many months. While face-to-face discussions about the 'D word' were infrequent, the rules of engagement, or rather disengagement, were established early on. There was no question of a messy court case, which mentioned the name of a third party. While she had every right to do so, the princess refused to play the adultery card, not only for the sake of their children but the monarchy. As with previous royal divorces, it was understood that they would wait for the statutory two-year period to elapse from their initial separation in December 1992 before initiating any permanent moves towards a legal split.

Throughout the summer of 1993, the princess was telling friends that she wanted a divorce, but that the decision had to come from him. At the same time the so-called Zenda group were working towards a reconciliation which, they claimed, the princess supported. Yet others in her circle described Diana as a woman waiting for Prince Charles to make up his mind about when, where and how their divorce would be arranged so that she could realize her dream and become a free woman. These contradictory signals from Diana's circle which resulted in a newspaper story saying that she was eager to divorce before the statutory two-year waiting period earned a sharp rebuke from her solicitors. 'We have received no instructions and have not been so engaged,' Lord Mishcon made known in a terse statement in August 1993.

In October 1993, after Prince Charles had brushed aside the olive branch proffered by the Zenda group, the royal couple met to discuss divorce and the princess's decision to withdraw from public life. He was nonplussed when she informed him that she was happy to wait for as long as necessary for a divorce, making it clear that on her part there was no hurry to part forever. 'That made him very jittery,' she remarked afterwards. Her 'wait-and-see' approach was based on advice from her lawyer Lord Mishcon. 'He just says to me, "Sit tight, they will come to us,"' she says. Again, when the prince returned from his successful Australian visit in February 1994, Diana phoned him to ask about the progress made on their divorce. She said that 9 December 1994 was approaching—the legal two-year period for an uncontested divorce—and wanted to make her feelings clear. The prince, anticipating her final departure, was initially enthusiastic as she outlined her plans. His mood quickly became downcast when she told him: 'I've made my mind up, I'm going to stay here.'

His frustration was apparent to his circle and on one occasion there was a heated exchange when intimates from both sides met at a private social occasion. Charles's friend, a West Country businessman, furiously demanded to know when 'that girl' was going to agree to a divorce and 'release' the prince. 'Never,' Diana's married girlfriend coolly replied: 'He has to ask for what he wants.'

In April 1994, the princess saw Jonathan Dimbleby, who, as she understood it, was acting as Charles's emissary. When he questioned her about why she had so far refused to press for a divorce, her concerns about the contents of the programme intensified. Dimbleby argued that it would make life easier for all concerned if she took up the issue. The princess replied that it was not for her to initiate divorce proceedings, contending that it would not serve her interests to resolve the issue prematurely. She believed that his camp wanted her to go quietly without the need to acknowledge publicly the fact that his extra-marital behaviour directly contributed to the marriage breakdown. When Prince Charles made his admission on television he was, intentionally or not, complying with one of her main demands. Her circle concluded that part of the purpose behind his public confession was an appeal to the princess to start proceedings. She had been given all the ammunition she wanted to divorce her husband without attracting public censure.

According to at least one report, the Queen summoned Prince Charles and Prince Andrew to Sandringham in the spring of 1995 to discuss the uncertainty surrounding their marriages, which many feel has harmed the reputation of the royal family. Indeed, Prince Edward has made it clear to friends that he would prefer his brothers to sort out their lives before he goes ahead with any plans to marry his long-time girlfriend, Sophie Rhys-Jones.

A friend, who regularly discussed the issue with the princess, explained the psychology behind her thinking:

She has always operated on the basis that it is not going to be her that causes the crisis because she feels that it would reflect badly on her. She has a pathological fear of being blamed. At the same time she would feel cheated out of all the effort and good work that she has been doing. At the end of the day she wants to leave her mark and if she just walks away she would be the loser. Everyone would say that she had not been able to take the pressure. The royal family would be sitting there and she would have endured thirteen years for nothing before opting out.

Yet her prudence, especially regarding access to the children, worried some of her friends, who watched with concern as she slipped on the familiar psychological garb of the victim, a helpless pawn unable to shape the course of events, rather than one of the central characters in the unfolding drama. If, they argued, she was genuinely searching for a new role and a new life then there was little point in marking time on the fringes of the royal family. The 'pack your bags and leave' school felt that the longer she vacillated, the more she compromised the chance of freedom which she so clearly longed for.

Perhaps her true feelings came to the surface the day she took Prince William for lunch at the fashionable family restaurant, Smollensky's Balloon, in central London, where one of the features of Sunday brunch is a magician who performs tricks at tables. Illusionist, John Styles, was on his best form at the royal table, the highpoint of his act being when he took Diana's wedding ring, placed it in a silk handkerchief and, with a flourish, made it vanish. Diana collapsed into a fit of laughter and cried: 'Good.'

As she knew, there was no magic wand that could erase the hurt of the last decade or easily resolve the constitutional and financial consequences of a royal divorce. Throughout the summer of 1994 a gentle head of steam began to rise. As divorce solicitor, Geoffrey Waters, explains in the appendix of this book, the financial wrangling is complicated by the fact that, while Prince Charles appears to be a rich man, he has relatively little capital in his own name, and the majority of money which provides his income is controlled by a twelve-man trust which administers the Duchy of Cornwall estates. This money is effectively locked up for the benefit of future heirs to the throne. Since the separation, for example, he has sold Highgrove, to the duchy. His adored country home cannot now be used as a bargaining chip, but the money produced from the sale, around £3 million, is on the table. This sum would only go partway to paying off the princess, as, according to Waters, she could well be entitled to a lump-sum payment of £15 million. With Prince Charles able to argue technical poverty, it is not inconceivable that, as with the divorces of Princess Anne and Princess Margaret, the Queen may be brought into negotiations, using funds drawn from her substantial private fortune to make up the balance.

During the summer months of 1994, Diana's meetings with Joseph Saunders, the discreet financial adviser who has for many years administered her Spencer trust fund, became more frequent as the financial package was pieced together. The princess indicated that she was happy to accept an annual allowance from the Duchy of Cornwall rather than a large one-off payment, her attitude reinforcing the notion that she was in no hurry to leave royal life. 'I'm happy to wait until William is eighteen,' she confided. However, after much discussion, the prince has agreed to buy two houses for the princess, one in central London, the other in the country. The property would not only be the home of Diana but also, from time to time, the future heir, Prince William, and as such would have to be acceptably regal in style and security. Suitable 'ambassadorial' accommodation in Kensington and Knightsbridge—the area where she would like to settle—is difficult to find, where prices range from £3 million to £6 million.

A country home is far less of a problem. A substantial property, with swimming pool, tennis courts, stables and rolling acres, could be purchased for £1 million. Her private secretary, Patrick Jephson, has already suggested that she looks for a country home in Wales, a country which she has grown to love, especially through her support for their rugby team. The welcome in the valleys would be all the more effusive as it would be the occasional base for the next Prince of Wales, Prince William. As opinion polls and the muted response to the investiture celebrations demonstrated, Prince Charles has not been a particularly popular Prince of Wales as the local population feel that he has done little to promote the interests of the principality. At the same time, since housing is much cheaper in Wales than other, more fashionable parts of Britain, Prince Charles would get off relatively lightly if Diana bought a home there. However, Jephson's suggestion does rather contradict the princess's dream of one day living in France.

While the prince's offer of two houses lies on the negotiating table, Diana has not yet started househunting. She does not want to be seen to be spending lavishly when she has a perfectly acceptable base at Kensington Palace. So Diana was annoyed and not a little confused when the prince complained about her £3,000 a week 'grooming' bill during a dinner party at the London home of a political socialite. Several days later his grumbles were conveniently passed on to two newspapers. Particular emphasis was laid on the word 'grooming,' with its connotation of frivolity and needless excess. The source, a member of Charles's camp, made it clear that the grooming bill did not include the princess's expenditure on clothes or her sons.

It was a ticklish editorial issue. Even with a little embroidery, the tapestry of Diana's day-to-day expenditure seemed too highly coloured to be true. It was estimated that she spent nearly £17,000 a year on manicures and pedicures, £700 a year on sun creams and £7,300 a year on New-Age therapies like massage and colonic irrigation. It simply did not add up, especially as her aides pointed out that most of her beauty and therapy treatments were paid for out of her own private bank account. Indeed, to spend anything remotely close to £160,000 Diana would have to spend at least ten hours a day undertaking therapy treatments. The princess herself was perplexed. When asked about the size of her annual grooming bill, she observed: 'I can't understand it, I don't even spend half that.' Even if that were the case, then a bill for Diana's private expenditure of £1,500 a week, although high, would not be ludicrously excessive, especially as much of her private spending is on presents and private donations to charities.

The story was seen by the princess and her circle as yet another salvo from Charles's camp to diminish Diana's public standing. Over the last two years, popular opinion has been an added dimension in the strategy of both the Prince and Princess of Wales. Since the separation both parties have deliberately tried to woo the public, knowing that, as legal and constitutional precedents for a divorced Prince and Princess of Wales are sketchy or non-existent, the court of public opinion would be the final arbiter as each side discreetly put their case. So Diana's future title, her financial settlement, and her ability to operate on the public stage would depend crucially upon her popularity. As the Duchess of York found to her cost, with an indifferent or downright hostile public, her relationship with the royal family, the government, charities and other bodies turned to ashes. The princess was not about to make the same mistakes as her sister-in-law. She was conscious that for every point she goes down in the polls, thousands of pounds could be shaved off the eventual settlement.

So in what seemed to an increasingly cynical public as a tit-for-tat gesture, the day after the exposure of Diana's 'grooming' bill, details emerged of her role in saving drowning tramp, Martin O'Donoghue, from the murky waters of a canal in London's Regent's Park. Diana, dressed in shorts and trainers, was returning from jogging in the park when her chauffeur-driven car was flagged down by a group of excited tourists, who told her that a man was in the water. She asked her driver to phone for help while she assisted Finnish student, Karl Kotila, who gave the tipsy Irishman the kiss of life after dragging him to the canal bank. She twice visited O'Donoghue at University College Hospital, on one occasion leaving a card with the message: 'Wishing you a speedy recovery—from Diana.' As in politics, a week is a long time in the royal family, seven days in which the princess was transformed from spendthrift to Saint Diana.

Amid these excursions and alarums during the summer of 1994, behind the arras of St James's Palace some quiet diplomacy was under way. A procession of constitutional experts such as Oxford academic, Vernon Bogdanor, and Professor David Starkey of the London School of Economics were sounded out about the likely constitutional consequences of a royal divorce. In the past the Church and the Establishment have got their own way in royal controversies. The abdication crisis of 1936 saw the effective exile of Edward VIII, later the Duke of Windsor, and the shabby treatment of the duchess, who was for a lifetime denied the title 'Her Royal Highness', a title she craved and legally was entitled to take. Again, the debate in the mid-1950s surrounding Princess Margaret's love for a divorcé, Group Captain Peter Townsend, resulted in her renunciation of the man she wanted to marry in favour of the teachings of the Church about the sanctity of marriage. Duty overcame personal wishes and desires in both cases. The public's sympathy for Edward VIII and for Princess Margaret were, on both occasions, brushed aside by the forces of reaction.

In the present royal imbroglio, the Establishment are on the defensive. There are few legal precedents to justify defying popular opinion. Diana's undoubted popularity—even during her retirement she is the most admired member of the royal family—is her most powerful card. Her enemies realize this and try to diminish her public standing at every turn.

The question is not, how can Diana accommodate herself to the monarchy, but how can the monarchy accommodate the princess so that the nation's regard for the institution remains untarnished. While not quite a race against time, the clock is ticking more loudly in Charles's camp than Diana's. A long, drawn-out separation works against the future king. While there is an assumption that the Queen will live to the same ripe old age as the Queen Mother, this is not inevitable. Under the 'if the Queen falls under a bus tomorrow' scenario, the Princess of Wales, even though separated, would be Queen. It would be an intolerable situation, resolved only by the princess renouncing her right to the throne in the settlement document currently under discussion. Ultimately it is in Charles's interests to resolve these outstanding questions.

However, the waiting game suits her needs at the moment, putting off the day when she leaves behind completely the royal family and all its trappings of prestige and privilege. She has already demonstrated that royal entitlements mean little to her by removing her accompanying retinue and by travelling under her maiden name, Diana Spencer. Indeed, her friends believe that, in the event of a divorce, she would revert to her maiden name, denying herself the right to have the appellation 'Her Royal Highness' before her name. While she has little truck with the style royalty gives, she knows that the position furnishes her with the status to promote causes and charities in which she believes. A divorce would mean that she would no longer be dusted with that special magic royalty confers, at a stroke radically diminishing her prestige and the opportunity to perform a useful service on the world stage.

It is a dilemma shrewdly noted by the Queen. While Prince Charles's camp is happy for the princess to leave the auditorium for ever, more conciliatory signals are emerging from Buckingham Palace. Diana was well-aware that 1995 was the 125th anniversary of the British Red Cross of which the Queen is president, herself vice-president. Diana agreed to sit for a portrait for the American artist Nelson Shanks on behalf of the charity and at the same time indicated an enthusiasm to take on the duties of patron for the anniversary year, acting as cheerleader for the celebrations. 'I'm coming back with a vengeance,' she told friends. 'You ain't seen nothing yet.' So it proved. In mid-November 1994, replete with police bodyguards, lady-in-waiting and other flunkeys, the princess was back centre-stage at Lancaster House where a gathering of notables, including Sir Angus Ogilvy, the Queen's private secretary, Sir Robert Fellowes and Overseas Aid Minister, Lynda Chalker, were present at the announcement of her return to public life under the Red Cross umbrella. A programme of visits, at home and abroad, was agreed, including a highly successful trip to Japan where she spoke several sentences in Japanese to an appreciative audience. The princess was back in the old routine, an irony which was not lost on her.

During her disastrous holiday in Spain in May 1994, she listened sympathetically as her unlikely knight, George Guy, poured his heart out about a failed love affair and his financial problems. As she was leaving she told him: 'Well, at least you're free.' Her response implied that she believes that she is still the 'PoW'—prisoner of Wales—her life constrained by the royal system, the detritus of a failed marriage and an eager and voracious mass media.

Certainly, she is a prisoner of her past, the patterns of her life formed in her childhood and coloured by an adult life celebrated as a living icon, a modern yet mysterious Madonna-figure, who reinvested the rather dull royal family with charisma and global appeal. In many ways the dream of freedom Diana is pursuing is illusory. While she will never escape her history, her challenge has been to use the lessons of her adult life to shape a more fulfilling future. She has proved time and again that she does not shrink from awkward choices, be it inside her marriage, her own family or her public life. The conventional solution would have been for her to endure an unhappy marriage for the sake of appearance and take a lover for the sake of her sanity. That journey has never been an option for the princess, who has often said that she knows in her heart that her path through life will be demanding and difficult.

Yet the last two years have seen something of a transformation. Before the separation, her friends saw a woman who was slowly dying inside. She was a pale shadow of the carefree teenage girl they once knew. The hard choices she has made have given her the one thing she never dared dream of. Hope. While she hovers on the brink of a new life, her thoughts are often tinged with understandable anger and a sense of betrayal. She feels saddened by the wasted years suffocating inside a miserable marriage, deceived by an unfaithful husband and an institution and social circle which colluded in a conspiracy of silence about his behaviour while expecting her to be a smiling but mute exotic, paraded in her gilded cage before the press and public. The new life she is slowly building is bringing a different kind of freedom, the freedom to be responsible for her own actions and decisions rather than forever deferring to or blaming someone else, be it her husband, royal courtiers or the media.

At present, many of the conditions for a divorce are in position. Her financial settlement is all but finalized, while the constitutional issues have been aired and a consensus reached. She could have petitioned for a divorce on 9 December 1994 but chose not to do so, her return to the royal fold and her reluctance to make the first move testimony to her willingness to adhere to the status quo. At the same time, the final parting between Camilla and Andrew Parker Bowles in January 1995 once more threw the royal separation in to the spotlight with courtiers saying privately that when the divorce settlement was finalized events would move very quickly. There was a feeling inside Prince Charles's camp that one of the reasons why Charles dithers over taking the final step is that he does not wish to upset his grandmother, the Queen Mother. However, this sentiment is dismissed by the Queen's former private secretary and confidante of the Queen Mother, Lord Charteris of Amisfield: 'The Queen Mother is aware that in her lifetime the Prince and Princess of Wales are going to divorce. She is quite prepared for it and she can and will withstand the shock. Divorce will clear the air and, yes, of course he will be king.' His robust pragmatism was in stark contrast with the vacillation of the two protagonists in this protracted drama. Indeed Diana's reluctance to initiate proceedings and her continued willingness to serve the Crown illustrates the dilemma she faces. If she wants to establish a career as a 'princess for the world' rather than the Princess of Wales, if she wants to remarry and have more children, then she must step down from the royal pedestal she has inhabited for the last decade, relinquishing her semi-divine status.

She is slowly, cautiously, and perhaps unconsciously, performing that striptease as the veils of mystery that have hitherto surrounded her fall. The regal fashions, which defined Diana's feminine mystique, have been left in the royal closet or given away. Her royal retinue, which described her status in society, has been dispersed while her love affair with the camera, which promoted her as the last of the silent screen goddesses, has ended literally in tears.

Contradictions abound. She longs to be ordinary, to be an anonymous woman in the street, yet she still enjoys the applause that fame and public acclamation bring. Her unassuming humanity, the consolation she brings to the victims of society, is sincere, but without a wider audience it remains well-meaning but ultimately ineffectual. As hard-headed charity officials know only too well, the real purpose of a princess is to bring publicity. The price of happiness, in the shape of a new husband and family, would cost her dearly by irrevocably altering the emotional balance between herself and her sons and, as important, her influence over the future king.

Her position is an unenviable one. It is her dearest wish to be accepted and appreciated for the person she is rather than the position she occupies. A woman who is admired for what she does rather than who she is. It is no easy task. As the criticism of her demonstrates, society is uneasy with powerful, self-willed women. The public prefers to admire the silent suffering of a Jackie Kennedy figure, treating with condemnatory suspicion articulate, ambitious women like Hillary Clinton or for that matter Madonna. As the twentieth-century's last icon, Diana is greatly loved. The public will not easily relinquish the image they have of her as the eternal virgin, perfect mother and androgynous sex symbol. They do not like their saints to have a shadow side.

The Princess of Wales will never be ordinary nor will she ever again be truly royal. She has vanquished the demons inside her marriage, and the royal system. Her challenge is to face the demons within as she embarks on a new life. As the princess once admitted to a close friend:

I had so many dreams as a young girl. I hoped for a husband to look after me, he would be a father figure to me, he would support me, encourage me, say 'well done' or 'that wasn't good enough'. I didn't get any of that. I couldn't believe it. I have learned much over the last years. From now on I am going to own myself and be true to myself. I no longer want to live someone else's idea of what and who I should be.

I am going to be me.

POSTSCRIPT

New World Princess

THESE DAYS IT IS A QUIET, almost monastic life. The daily bread comes from Harrods at a thirty-three per cent discount—the water is designed by Volvic and the cloistered atmosphere at Kensington Palace is broken only by the shrill sound of the telephone, an instrument which is at once her confessional, her best friend and her occasional doom. She worships daily at the temple of her body, rigorous in her adherence to a Spartan diet of exercise, massage, therapy and medication. Often the Princess of Wales is in bed by eight. Alone. Her solitary existence, largely self-imposed, concerns her rapidly dwindling circle of friends. 'Such loneliness, she doesn't know who she can trust,' says Lucia Flecha de Lima, Diana's surrogate mother, to whom Diana has fled in America during

221

the storms of the last year. Diana's seclusion, however, comes with a high price tag; with a private secretary, two secretaries, a chauffeur, two butlers, two dressers, a chef, two housemaids and a kitchen maid, the annual wages' bill alone for her staff is £150,000.

The daily routine rarely varies. Her day starts promptly at seven in the morning when one of her dressers, usually Helen Walsh, knocks on her bedroom door, opens her curtains and puts a glass of mineral water and several tiny plastic cups containing her assortment of pills and medicines by her bedside. She dresses quickly, slipping on a leotard and sneakers before eating a light breakfast in the first-floor dining room: pink grapefruit, home-made muesli or granary toast, or fresh fruit and yoghurt, and coffee. As is traditional with members of the royal family, she eats alone. Even when William and Harry are at home they still eat in the nursery. She flicks through the *Daily Mail*, *Daily Telegraph* and *Daily Express* which are laid out for her perusal. If she knows that anything unpleasant is likely to appear she asks her butlers, Harold Brown or Paul Burrell, to cancel that day's order. Staff know from experience that if she has a bad press that day, they are in for a hard time.

Breakfast takes little longer than ten minutes and then she departs for her daily workout at the exclusive £1,200-a-year Chelsea Harbour Club, a two-mile drive away. Some days she works out with her fitness teacher, Carol Ann Brown, on others she works through her routine alone. Occasionally Carol Ann joins her at Kensington Palace. She never showers at her club, preferring to change at home, away from curious eyes—and possible camera lenses. If the police on the gate at Kensington Palace are on their toes they will have alerted the butlers to her arrival before her green Audi scrunches up the gravel drive. Then, either Paul or Harold will be standing by the open door. If not, she opens it herself with her own key.

Around nine o'clock her flamboyant hairdresser, Sam McKnight, puts in an appearance. He is one of the few men in her life who can keep the princess waiting—and still keep her smiling. McKnight, who specializes in styling models for magazine photo shoots, has been known to breeze in an hour late after a heavy night on the town. But she forgives him because he regales her with all the gossip about the supermodels. It was through McKnight that Diana met Linda Evangelista, a model she has admired from afar, and has since met on several occasions. As McKnight, invariably dressed in his trademark Vivienne Westwood tartan jacket and leather trousers, attends her hair, the princess is busy on her bedroom phone. Friends know that early morning is a good time to catch Diana. She is usually chatty, eager to share her anxieties about, say, an awkward meeting or a tricky domestic problem. On the other hand, she may want to express her irritation at some inaccurate story about her in the day's press. It is at this time she can be light-hearted and gay. By evening when the events of the day have exhausted her and her emotional batteries are depleted, making conversation can be, as one friend notes, 'like pushing glue uphill'.

When McKnight has departed, Diana drifts downstairs to her sitting room to open her private mail using a steel letter-opener adorned with her initial 'D' crest. As she browses through her correspondence, her private secretary Patrick Jephson, accompanied by her two secretaries, Nicki Cockle and Victoria Mendham, arrives to discuss the business of the day. Even during her withdrawal from public life, there was a mound of correspondence, much of it from her charities. Since her decision to spearhead the 125th anniversary celebrations of the Red Cross and to undertake occasional public duties, her office is busier. Her frequent visits to America and the official tours of, for instance, Hong Kong, Japan and France, barely impinge upon the domestic rhythm of her life and these morning meetings rarely take more than half-an-hour.

From about ten o'clock, she likes to phone friends. Regular callers include Lord Palumbo, her lawyer Lord Mishcon and, rather surprisingly given past hostilities, her stepmother, Raine, and also the Duchess of York. If she is feeling depressed or bored or lonely, she goes shopping to cheer herself up. Diana shops a lot. She is seen so often on Kensington High Street that it has been nicknamed Kensington Di Street. For a woman renowned for her neatness, it is not surprising that there is an orderliness about her shopping habits. She carries a leatherbound notebook to keep a record of her purchases, which, under the terms of the separation, the Duchy of Cornwall pays for. 'It's great spending money on his account,' she jokes with friends.

The princess buys clothes for the princes. It is always two of everything as the parents have agreed that William and Harry should have identical wardrobes for their time at Highgrove or Kensington Palace. For her overseas visits, Diana will buy a couple of new outfits, but the days when designers came to Kensington Palace with swatches of samples and sketches are long gone. She knows exactly where to go and what she wants, visiting, for instance, Manolo Blahnik for shoes and asking them to send several samples to her home so that she can make a final choice. Then there are the endless gifts for official visits, charities, staff and other bodies that come in to the princess' purview. Last Christmas, for example, she gave each of her staff a solid silver cup from Garrards, engraved 'From Diana 1994' as a thankyou gift. She goes to Garrards for silver photoframes, Andrew Soo for leather gifts, like wallets and handbags, and Smythson Frank of New Bond Street for the endless supplies of paper and envelopes she needs. While she chooses the style, design and crest for her purchases, her two butlers are dispatched to pick them up. Staff know if she has been pestered by photographers because she can return to Kensington Palace in 'a real bate'.

Besides the shopping trips, there are weekly visits to see her therapist Susie Orbach at her north London home or, if Sam McKnight is away, she drives to hairdresser Daniel Galvin's West End salon. On Thursday mornings, she travels to nearby Beauchamp Place for a colonic irrigation session with Chryssie Fitzgerald. For a time her husband, fitness instructor Keith Rodriques, gave her kick-boxing lessons at Kensington Palace. The night before a session, the butlers moved furniture in the drawing room to give the sparring partners space. Diana, wearing red boxing gloves and white Reebok training shoes, then spent an hour punching the arm pads worn by her trainer. It improved her physique, agility and helped her release some of the anger she feels.

Lunch is rather less strenuous. When she sees friends, she normally eats out, meeting at restaurants like Mortons, Launceston Place, Le Caprice or Kaspia, a caviar house. Since a certain coolness developed in her friendship with Mara Berni—another former honorary surrogate mother—she has not been to her one-time favourite watering hole, San Lorenzo in Beauchamp Place. Most of the time, however, she eats lunch alone at Kensington Palace. Her needs are simple: a glass of Volvic water, a pasta dish or a humble jacket potato topped with caviar or foie gras, with yoghurt to follow. Under the guidance of her masseur Stephen Twigg, she tries to stick to the Hay diet, an eating formula which counsels against combining carbohydrate and protein at the same meal.

When she entertains girlfriends, she will usually open a bottle of Chablis, and eat a fish dish like scallop mornay with saffron rice, followed by sorbet. For male friends, she serves meat, usually lamb cutlets, and when it is a business lunch, and Mike Whitlam of the Red Cross is a regular, it will be a three-course affair with full butler service. As they wait for the princess before lunch, guests can flick through the magazines on display, like *Vogue, Harpers & Queen, Tatler* and, surprisingly, the socialist journal *New Statesman*. Staff remark that when a business lunch is planned, the celebrity magazine *Hello!* is taken from the top and put on the bottom of the pile. However, there is rarely any need for this subterfuge, as she entertains infrequently. In the last year she has seen friends like Kate Menzies and Catherine Soames, advisers like Lord Rothschild and TV personality Clive James—he suggested that she learn a couple of sentences of Japanese before her visit there in spring 1995—the pop singer George Michael and film-maker Sir Richard Attenborough. Royal visitors are a rarity. During the thirteen years she has lived at Kensington Palace, Diana's next-door neighbours, Prince and Princess Michael of Kent, have only been for drinks once and the Queen has called on the princess for tea twice, and that was a decade ago. Only the Duchess of Kent and Sarah Chatto, the daughter of Princess Margaret, have ever lunched with the princess. When the Duke of Gloucester said that the Windsors are not a 'dropping in' family, he was not exaggerating.

Lunch is over by 2.15 pm prompt. The days when Diana, her sister Sarah and Kate Menzies would take a bottle of white wine downstairs to the princess' huge wardrobes and try on clothes are a rapidly fading memory. It's back to the telephone or perhaps a spot more shopping. If she is scheduled to perform an official engagement, she has been known to take a gulp of vodka before facing the world, such is her reluctance to return to the old routine. When she returns to Kensington Palace it is not uncommon for her to mock the absurdities of the event with any member of staff within earshot. Alternatively, she may receive official visitors connected to her charities or regiments, or spend an hour or so catching up with correspondence, which arrives each day in a red plastic bag. Sometimes she visits her offices at St James's Palace—she recently ordered secretary Victoria Mendham to buy a new china tea service because she was sick of the old one—or she drives to Ludgrove to see the boys play in their school sports teams. During the summer she spends hours sitting on a bench in the garden, Sony Walkman clamped to her head, engrossed in the latest blockbuster novel. Unlike Prince Charles who loves to take a picnic outside on a sunny day, Diana always dines indoors. Between four and five in the afternoon she might retire to bed, either for a siesta, to read or write letters to friends.

While she is resting, there is a quiet hum of activity in her apartment as her butlers, Paul and Harold, field the constant telephone enquiries from charities, St James's Palace and the multifarious official bodies which have dealings with the princess. One of their most ticklish problems is when Tiggy Legge-Bourke rings with details about the boys' movements. Tiggy is reluctant to speak to the princess direct, and that feeling is entirely mutual. Instead, messages are relayed via the butlers. Staff know that there is hell to pay if either parent is misinformed or remains in ignorance about any aspect of the boys' lives. 'It is the only time Diana ever really hits the roof,' observes one of her circle. Again, if there is a photograph in the newspapers of Tiggy with the boys, staff know that they are in for a rough day. Indeed it is hard to escape the conclusion that this mutual antipathy between Diana and Tiggy makes Tiggy virtually bomb-proof in Prince Charles's eyes. At the staff Christmas party held in the crypt at London's Guildhall, Tiggy gaily wrapped twinkling festive lights around her boss' neck. 'No other member of staff would have dared be so intimate with the Prince of Wales,' remarked one member of staff.

Twice a week, at five o'clock sharp, Dr Mary Loveday, who runs a clinic specializing in allergy and clinical ecology, arrives and spends an hour with the princess to deal with her 'lifestyle management'. For the last three years Dr Loveday, who has many other well-heeled clientele, has counselled the princess on her numerous medical difficulties. With her nightly sleeping pills, vitamins and the drug Prozac to counter her bulimia, the princess' life is spent on an even, if rather subdued, keel. During her struggle with bulimia, an eating disorder where sufferers binge and then vomit, her butlers regularly ordered the royal kitchen to leave bowls of custard, rice pudding and other nursery food in the fridge for the princess so that she could indulge in her craving for a late-night feast. The end of that roller-coaster dietary regime is a sure indication of her progress towards a calmer lifestyle. Her only indulgence these days are endless bars of chocolates or Holland and Barrett fruit-and-nut bars. Her chauffeur, Steve David, regularly disgorges the wrappers from the door pockets of her Audi.

Her inner peace is assisted by the sure touch of her masseur Stephen Twigg, who for a while left her to write a book but has since returned because, as Diana remarked, 'He has the best hands in London.' He arrives at around six in the evening after Dr Loveday has departed and spends an hour twice a week caring for Diana's body and discussing her problems, often suggesting ways of self-improvement.

When not involved in medical consultation or massage, it is at this time of day that the princess likes to make private visits away from the eyes of royal staff and police. She may ask for a picnic supper hamper to be made up and then go off on her own, usually to see her sister Sarah at her home in Earls Court where they can meet mutual friends in relative secrecy. On other occasions, she has been known to wear a headscarf and dark glasses in an attempt at a disguise. Once this subterfuge rather badly backfired when, the princess, smartly followed by her friends Lucia Flecha de Lima and Mara Berni, in similar attire, marched in through the front entrance of the Albany apartment block in London's Piccadilly to see her actor friend, Terence Stamp. As the scene rather resembled a bad Hollywood spy movie, passing paparazzi were soon on the case and waiting outside.

Such excitements are few and far between. Her normal domestic pattern is more mundane. Often she retires to bed to eat a light supper of pasta, salmon or scallops, and yoghurt from a wicker tray. While water is her staple tipple she has been known to drink the occasional glass of champagne as she catches up on the latest soaps. Occasionally she will go out to the movies with a couple of girlfriends, taking in an evening show at her regular haunts, Whiteleys or the Odeon Kensington. Sometimes she goes to the opera or the theatre, but, unlike Prince Charles who regularly makes midnight visits to art galleries like the Tate and the National, Diana is no night owl.

Her weekends, if anything, are quieter than her weekdays. While many of her friends decant for the country, the princess is content to stay at Kensington Palace. In the last eighteen months, for example, she has spent only two weekends away, one with her friend Julia Samuel, and one with Lord Palumbo and his family. Instead, the princess spends most of her Saturday mornings at the Chelsea Harbour Club. She leaves around 8.30am for a game of tennis or coaching and regularly joins the England rugby captain Will Carling for breakfast. The sporting pin-up, who recently married a TV presenter, has become something of a royal favourite, privy to royal secrets and high on the invitation list for functions at Kensington Palace. In turn, he asked Diana if she wanted to let the princes join the England team for a practice session at Twickenham shortly before the Grand Slam decider game with Scotland. The princess, who warms to those who give her sons their attention, was delighted to see the enjoyment of William and Harry as they played with their sporting heroes.

After lunch, she may pop out to the cinema, or go for a thirty-minute jog in Kensington Palace Gardens. At least once a month she spends the afternoon with the Duchess of York and her daughters, Princesses Beatrice and Eugenie, at their home in Sunningdale, Berkshire. A quiet Saturday evening watching television with a light supper is the norm. She is a fan of mawkish Saturday night hospital drama *Casualty* and has never been known to miss an instalment of the dating game, *Blind Date*, hosted by Cilla Black.

She likes to arrange social dates herself, but only when she feels no one is watching. On Sunday afternoon at four o'clock her staff are dismissed and it is then that she entertains her friends with a reasonable degree of privacy. Only the police know the comings and goings at apartments eight and nine. In March 1995, for example, art dealer Oliver Hoare spent much of the afternoon and early evening with his royal friend in spite of the continuing speculation in the media about the exact nature of their friendship.

The reclusive atmosphere of Diana's home—one royal employee dubbed it 'Bleak House'—is leavened when the boys spend a weekend with their mother. In fact the only times there are ever raised voices are when the boys are around. If there is something in the press she doesn't want the boys to read she tells the staff to hide the newspapers from the young princes. They have got wise to this trick and now spend the mornings searching high and low for the banned tabloids—much to their mother's consternation and annoyance. Under the terms of the separation the princess sees the boys alternate weekends when school holidays allow. When it is her turn, she picks them up from Ludgrove on Friday afternoon, pops in to a local sweetshop and then drives back to London. Tea is in the nursery—roast chicken or pork are favourites—with their nanny Olga Powell. Diana will sometimes join them for a typical supper of baked beans and potato waffles. On Friday evening they use Prince Charles's former study as a television room where they sit glued to the latest action movies. The princess installed The Movie Channel on Sky, the satellite network, so that they wouldn't miss their favourites. (One weekend the boys were taken by their nanny and detectives to see the Arnold Schwarzenegger adventure, *Last Action Hero.* Even though Harry was well under age, he was so keen to see his screen hero that his minders smuggled him in.) Often the princes will watch a video like *Rambo* rented from the local store after they have had supper and a bath. Or they may play the computer game Nintendo, a pastime Prince Charles disapproves of, probably because Harry can beat him. Then between nine and ten they go to bed but not before they troop downstairs in their red and blue striped pyjamas and matching dressing-gowns to kiss their mother good-night.

On Saturday and Sunday mornings, at around 8.30 am, William and Harry have breakfast of apple juice, boiled or scrambled eggs and cereal with their nanny. The princess keeps to her own schedule even when they are around and it is left to nanny Olga to supervise dressing. While William is easy to please and will wear what is chosen for him, Harry is a nightmare. He is very fussy about his attire and is forever chopping and changing. However the prince is a military fanatic—his bedroom is full of army paraphernalia—and spends half his life dressed in camouflage gear, walking round the apartment with a toy gun and talking to his elder brother or detective via a real walkie-talkie.

When the boys are ready, they may join their mother at the Chelsea Harbour Club where they are learning to play short tennis, or stay and ride their BMX bikes around the palace. For a time, they lobbied their mother to buy them a dog but she resisted the idea; instead they make do with feeding the ducks in Kensington Palace Gardens. They let off steam in vigorous water-pistol fights with members of staff and the police, spray each other with hosepipes from the garage—the bane of the chauffeur's life—or have pitched water-bomb battles with their school-friends who may join them for the day. Harry's favourite pastime is to spend the morning at a go-cart circuit in Berkshire. Those who have watched the budding sportsman say that he is quite fearless, eager to run William in to the ground. 'Harry is far and away the better athlete and in a tussle William will always give way,' notes a family friend. The young prince was delighted when an Arab millionaire gave the youngsters a miniature MG sports car to play with, but that mood soon changed when the princess returned it saying that it was 'inappropriately expensive'. As a result of Harry's athletic prowess and the constant sibling rivalry, William prefers to go horseriding or shooting with his schoolfriends where he is not constantly frustrated by his inability to better his younger brother. While William is the more ponderous and serious, Harry is the more nimble and impish, in sport and conversation. When the young prince was choosing his room at his new school, Eton College, William loyally stated that he would like one with a view of Windsor Castle, 'granny's castle' as he called it. Instantly Harry, grimacing in the direction of the fire-damaged pile, quipped, 'What's left of it.' Yet while Harry teases his elder brother mercilessly—his knobbly knees are a regular target—he needs him desperately. When William has had enough of his younger brother and has gone off on his own, Harry will run round the palace apartments calling his name.

On Sunday afternoon the boys go back to school and Kensington Palace returns to its customary peace. Beneath this outward calm, there are underlying tensions which reflect much about the changing character of the princess as she struggles to find a new sense of direction and purpose in her life. Inevitably, her inward, some may say self-indulgent, lifestyle, as well as her self-imposed isolation, places an emotional burden on her staff. She confides and relies on them in a way which is totally at odds with other members of the royal family, especially Prince Charles, who clearly understand the unspoken demarcation line of the 'green baize door'. Staff are staff, royalty are royalty, and never the twain shall meet. Everyone knows their place. The Queen would no more dream of seeing the chef in his kitchen at Buckingham Palace than he would expect an invitation to tea.

At the same time, experienced royal retainers know that if for any reason they left royal service prematurely, their royal employers wouldn't give their departure—or demise—a second thought. When Prince Charles's one-time bodyguard, John McLean, famously quipped, 'I would kill for the buggers but I wouldn't die for them,' he was articulating the view that, ultimately, loyalty counts for naught with royalty. It makes for an impersonal but smooth-running status quo where staff never anticipate thanks or gratitude nor do they expect interference or interest in their personal lives.

The princess, however, treats her staff as human beings, regularly building emotional bonds with them, which in itself creates tensions. 'She is easy-going but you have to play her game and the rules change all the time,' commented one former retainer. She frequently goes behind the 'green baize door', befriending staff, especially at times of personal difficulty. When her chef Darren McGrady recently divorced, the princess was on hand with words of consolation and advice. She took time to visit Prince Charles's former valet Ken Stronach in the London Clinic when he suffered severe spinal problems and she was constantly at the side of her former bodyguard Graham Smith in his fight against cancer. The princess takes an interest too in the lives of staff in other royal households. She visited the late Vic Fletcher, one-time Yeoman of the Silver Pantry at Buckingham Palace, when he was in hospital, and she regularly sends letters to servants who are ill or have suffered some personal misfortune.

The princess is wont to roam around the staff quarters at Kensington Palace, drifting in, uninvited, to the staff room, picking up correspondence or leafing through private paperwork. Her unbidden curiosity is an echo of her childhood days when she and her brother Charles used to rummage through their father's desk drawers to find letters between the late earl and his future wife, Raine Spencer. It is not uncommon for staff who are in the middle of a private conversation to find the princess hovering nearby or to find her in the kitchens 'helping out'. As her offers of assistance mean in practice getting in the way, her staff see this behaviour as her desire to see a friendly face in her isolated position while catching up on the latest gossip, be it about herself or other members of the royal family. These actions come as no surprise to those who know the princess well. As one commented, 'It is a classic case of insecurity. Coming from a broken home she finds it very difficult to trust those around her. Yet, when she does know people for a long time she cannot handle the relationship. That makes it very tricky for her staff.'

Her deep-seated insecurity, need for approval and inability to sustain relationships helps make for a very edgy atmosphere at Kensington Palace. It is hard for staff to gauge who is 'in' and who is 'out' in her circle as she chops and changes so frequently. So, for instance, one week she sings the praises of Prime Minister John Major, the next he is *persona non grata*. The same is true of those deemed to be in her inner circle. Thus the Duchess of York, Raine Spencer, Kate Menzies—she fell out with Kate during a recent skiing trip to Lech in Austria and consequently missed her thirty-fifth birthday party—Lucia Flecha de Lima, 'too fussy and wants to organize my life' and restaurateur Mara Berni, 'too possessive', have all fallen foul of the princess at one time or other. It is noticeable that such is her distance from her family that when her brother Earl Spencer decided on a trial separation from his wife Victoria during her treatment for anorexia, the princess, in common with the rest of the public, didn't learn about it until six weeks after the couple had agreed to part.

Staff at Kensington Palace know that they have displeased the royal personage in some way when she simply ignores them. 'It makes them very uncomfortable and jumpy,' says one retainer. Her dresser, like Prince Charles's valet, is the bellwether for her daily moods. A raised eyebrow from Helen Walsh is all the warning other staff need to keep their heads down. Unlike Prince Charles who has a reputation for throwing anything to hand at errant staff—books, china ornaments, pens and on one memorable occasion a ceremonial sword dating back to George V which whizzed past the head of one hapless valet—the princess shows her displeasure with a cutting comment or terse manner. Her tetchiness can be predicted and is usually the result of nervousness. Before an official engagement, a speech and especially a visit to a member of the royal family, she becomes very jittery and is apt to be uncharacteristically brusque. There was little seasonal cheer at Kensington Palace for a couple of days before Christmas as the princess psyched herself up to meet the rest of the royal family at Sandringham for a flying twenty-four-hour visit.

The recent departure of two long-serving members of staff has merely exacerbated the mood of nervy apprehension. When the royal couple separated, Paul and Maria Burrell who worked at Highgrove as butler and housemaid were transferred to Kensington Palace, with their two children Alexander and Nicholas. While the Burrells were unhappy about the disruption, they settled down well and soon the Queen's former footman was one of Diana's favourites. His sons played with William and Harry, joining them for a day out at Thorpe Park theme park, for instance, while he and Maria became, for a time, royal confidantes. Such was her friendship with the Burrells, that the princess attended a fancy-dress party to celebrate Maria's fortieth birthday and joined the rest of the staff in a conga dance, grabbing the waist of Paul Burrell, who was dressed as a Roman soldier.

When dresser Helen Roach left, the princess asked Maria, then a housemaid, if she would take on the position. It was agreed that she would take the position for a year's trial. Unfortunately the arrangement did not work out as well as either side had hoped, and in January 1995 there was a mutual parting of ways. Two months after Maria Burrell left to spend more time with her children, the princess' staff were disturbed by another departure. In March, her chef Mervyn Wycherley, who had worked for the Queen, Prince Charles and the princess for nearly twenty years, was told by Diana's private secretary, Patrick Jephson, that his services were no longer required because of the princess' reduced workload. The episode brought home to her staff that however informal and friendly the princess may be, the uncertainty and indecision about her private and public life have inevitable repercussions. Her vow in autumn 1994 that she was going to be 'back with a vengeance' has turned out to be far more low key. 'We never know from one day to the next whether she is going to stay inside the royal family or go and live in America. It is very unsettling,' commented one of her circle. Her flirtation with America—she made her fifth flying visit over Easter 1995 in almost as many months—derives as much from her friendship with Lucia Flecha de Lima, who has introduced her to a new circle of appreciative socialites, as her need to shed those who have become too close to her. She searches for pastures—and plaudits—anew.

At the same time, her transatlantic love affair is in something of a royal tradition. As several royal outsiders have discovered, when life sours on one continent, they are assured of an expansive and adulatory welcome on the other side of the Atlantic. Effectively exiled from Britain, the Duke and Duchess of Windsor spent many a month on the Palm Beach cocktail circuit; Princess Michael of Kent chose to lick her wounds in a California retreat following the scandal of her secret friendship with a Texan property millionaire, while the Duchess of York, seen as the black sheep of the royal family and blamed by many for their present predicament, spends as much time as possible with her American allies. The Duchess of York, for example, chose to launch her *Budgie* range of children's books and memorabilia at F A O Schwarz in New York rather than at a London store.

So, the Princess of Wales, wearied by the constant sniping of the British media and worn down by Palace in-fighting, has increasingly made America, if not her physical home, certainly a place of spiritual refuge. She likes the unaffected openness of the American people and the relatively friendly welcome she receives from their media. 'It's an egalitarian society,' she remarked to friends, 'they accept you for what you are, not who you are. I like that.' Like many a British superstar before her, the princess feels comfortable with a culture where success and celebrity are not dirty words. She feels that where the British are grudging, the Americans are generous with their applause. It is a sublime historical irony that the nation which fought a war to rid itself of the yoke of monarchy now welcomes royalty with an enthusiasm which is found only occasionally in England.

Her friendship with Liza Minnelli, her admiration for Hillary Clinton and her support for Elizabeth Glaser, the wife of the television actor Michael Glaser, during her long battle against AIDS, revealed a princess at ease with the cosmopolitan society and the social issues with which American high society is concerned. Such is her fascination with America that it has given rise to speculation that she would one day settle in America. According to the gossips, she was considering at one time buying apartments in New York, Florida and California while being wooed by every billionaire businessman—for a time Teddy Forstman was favourite—in Manhattan.

However, the princess is in no hurry to move on, aware that her primary responsibility is that of mother to the future king. When William comes of age, all that may change. In autumn 1995, he is bound for Eton, and the princess has toyed with the idea of buying a house in Berkshire so that she can be near him. However, before his schooling is ended, he is likely to follow the example of his father and uncles and spend some time at a school in a Commonwealth country. Lakefield school in Ontario, Canada, which played host to Prince Andrew, has already indicated a readiness to accept the future king as a student. This would give the princess the perfect excuse to spend extended vacations in America.

Diana is certainly tempted. She is rather flattered by the American public's perception of her as the 'new Jackie O', acutely aware that her very public loneliness, her style and grace carries echoes of the late, much-lamented First Lady. Diana has discussed with friends a possible future life in America (although it must be said that she has done the same about living in France). For the last two Christmases she has quietly taken flight to the States and she was delighted that her New Year skiing trip to Vail, Colorado was relatively photographer-free. Again, when Prince Charles's biography was published in autumn 1994, Diana headed for Washington, recharging her emotional batteries at a high-octane dinner party attended by First Lady Hillary Clinton and Colin Powell, commander of the Gulf forces. As she left the nation's capital she pointedly told a Brazilian reporter: 'I hope we can now look to the future and not hang on to the past.'

Unfortunately the princess has learned to her cost that she can run but she cannot hide. Even as she has shrouded herself in a veil of seclusion at Kensington Palace and sought sanctuary in America, the ghosts of her past have returned to haunt and embarrass her. As she lay in the sun in Martha's Vineyard where she joined her friend Lucia Flecha de Lima for a holiday in August 1994, her former riding instructor Captain James Hewitt was regurgitating his colourful memories about his relationship with the princess. He boasted of a six-year love affair, torrid weekends spent at his Devon farmhouse and a torrent of anguished *billet doux* she sent him while he was serving with his regiment during the Gulf war. According to the breathless account, she initiated their illicit affair one evening after dinner at Kensington Palace, where 'with the ease of a dancer practising a well-worn routine, she stood up, walked across to him and slipped sideways on to his lap'. Her staff, in fact, point out that, according to records, he never visited Kensington Palace in the evening.

The revelations, written in the style of a Harlequin romance, were greeted with a mixture of mirth and incredulity. The queen of the romantic novelists, Barbara Cartland, was so aghast at the appalling prose style that, tongue firmly in cheek, she threatened to sue if commentators compared this tome to her own fictional confections. By turns anxious, angry and hurt by Hewitt's duplicity, Diana sought the advice of her lawyer, Lord Mishcon, about taking legal action. He was cautious, arguing that a lawsuit would only attract more publicity and that in any case the lack of evidence to prove his story spoke for itself. It did not stop her telling anyone who would listen that Hewitt was a dreamer who had exploited her friendship by fabricating an intimacy which never existed. Noticeably, it was her stepmother Raine, now Countess Chambrun, who proved a stalwart supporter, keeping her spirits high with a stream of sympathetic telephone calls. 'I've never felt stronger,' the princess observed, as she watched the media squall rapidly abate.

Indeed it wasn't long before Diana began to see the funny side of a book which many looked on as an unintentional comic masterpiece: an overweening ego and a florid prose style run riot. When an acquaintance mentioned the media hunt for Hewitt, who was hiding in France with his mother, she retorted wryly: 'They are looking for Hewitt, wait until I get my hands on him.' Yet, beneath the surface amusement—she smiled when she was told that the book was for sale in an Oxfam charity shop for 50 pence just twenty-four hours after publication—she felt a simmering sense of betrayal at a lonely Army officer who, by her own admission, she had dressed, cosseted and mothered. Robustly she categorically denied his assertion that they were lovers saying: 'It is all fantasy. He wanted to have sex but I never let it happen. I am a married woman.'

According to Hewitt, he was the Professor Higgins character who had given Diana voice lessons, drafted her speeches, cured her bulimia and given her the will to carry on her royal duties. She, in the meantime, would wear red nail varnish—his favourite— on official duties just to let him know that she was thinking about him. The princess' circle, who had watched Hewitt's behaviour over many years, was openly sceptical of his claim. They recalled that in the mid-1980s Captain Hewitt was one of a number of Life Guard officers, including Major David Waterhouse, who formed part of her social circle. 'He was', says a friend, 'easy on the eye and easier on the brain.' A man of immense charm and savoir-faire, he helped her overcome her fear of horseriding and, more importantly, struck up a jolly rapport with Princes William and Harry, giving them piggyback rides and indulging in other horseplay. 'She saw in him someone fulfilling the role of the father she would have liked Prince Charles to have been. The boys liked him and that was a great plus,' recalls a friend. 'Certainly in the early stages of their relationship in 1987 when Diana was at the lowest ebb in her life there was a sexual chemistry between them. Speaking to her around that time I know that if they had an affair, or flirtation, it was very short-lived. Certainly she always said that she never had the strength of feeling for him that he had for her. She was married and still held out hope that the marriage could be mended.'

Evidence that Hewitt and Diana may have enjoyed a short-lived fling was alleged later to the *News of the World* when the former housekeeper at Highgrove, Wendy Berry, attempted to sell her diaries. It was reported that she recalled how Hewitt had come to stay at Highgrove one weekend when Prince Charles was in Norfolk with the Queen. When she went to change Diana's sheets she found that they were virtually untouched while Hewitt's in his first-floor bedroom down the corridor were dishevelled. 'As I stripped off the sheets it became quite obvious that two people had slept in them. There were strands of long hair on one of the pillows and evidence some sort of activity had taken place on the bottom sheet,' she claimed.

Whether they enjoyed more than a flirtatious friendship or an affair, what is clear is that Hewitt quickly used his royal association to gain social approval inside his regiment. Diana's riding instructor was all too painfully aware that in the snobbish hierarchy of the Life Guards officer class, his modest social and financial background meant that he was always on the outside looking in. His friendship with the princess was his ticket to social acceptance. It wasn't long before Diana heard that she was being treated like a mess trophy, Hewitt and other officers jealously vying with one another to see who was the closest to the princess. Like so many Regency fops, these modern-day dandies would contact Diana with derogatory gossip about their rivals, much to her amusement. On one occasion she remarked that she never realized that men could be bitchier than women until she had seen Life Guards in action.

Yet, in spite of his appeal as an amusing companion, the princess realized that here was a man obsessed. She was not alone in that assessment. Fellow officers and Buckingham Palace courtiers knew him as something of a royal groupie, a young man desperate for a position at the Royal Court as an equerry or some other military functionary. He was also a man consumed with self-pity, forever moaning about his lonely life in Devon where he lived with his mother. During his frequent phone calls to the princess, he continually complained about his failure to find true love. In turn, Diana encouraged him to find a girlfriend—hardly the words of a woman consumed by breathless passion. Yet on one occasion he spoke to her from a hand-held phone while he was in the bath with a woman—Diana told friends that she could clearly hear them splashing and Hewitt's girlfriend giggling in the background.

In fact Hewitt had a string of lovers at the very time he boasted of his alleged royal affair. Former girlfriend, Sarah Portley, revealed on American television, which was later quoted in the *Daily Express*, that she realized that Hewitt was enjoying his fling with her at the same time as wooing his former girlfriend Emma Stewardson, as well as claiming a romance with the princess. She said wryly, 'James was such a liar but he could always make you forget your doubts about him by giving you his full attention.' His boastfulness and his constant calls meant that, as far as the princess was concerned, he had become a nuisance who had long outstayed his welcome. During the Gulf War, where he served as a tank commander, letters she had sent him—she wrote to several other Army friends serving in the conflict—surfaced in the media and he seemed to throw caution to the wind by using the *Daily Mail* correspondent's satellite telephone to call the princess from the war zone. She was further astonished by his cheek when he asked her to instruct Buckingham Palace to handle media enquiries about his exploits. His frequent protestations of love—on one occasion he asked her to marry him, on another he assured her that he would stand by her if she ever became pregnant—propelled the princess in to action. In December 1991, she drove to his Devon home to warn him off and to ask him to remain discreet about their relationship.

Now firmly on the outside of her circle, his military career also over, Hewitt was a bitter and virtually penniless young man. When he did speak to Diana, she noticed that the nature of the conversations had altered. He was now fishing for information, but she refused to believe, as was later proved, that he was selling gossip to a downmarket tabloid, the Sunday *People*. When she asked him why he seemed to be quoted so much in that particular newspaper he explained that he had been asked to comment on polo. Diana drily replied: 'I would have thought their readers would know more about the mint than the game.' In August 1992 when she was told that he had consulted the notorious publicist Max Clifford about selling his story, Diana refused to believe it, pointing out that he had taken out a writ against the *Sun* newspaper concerning its allegation that he had had a 'physical relationship' with her. Yet two years later, Hewitt, now unemployed, the man who had once been prepared to swear an oath in court that his royal relationship was purely platonic, was now writing about an intense and torrid sexual liaison. True to form, Hewitt denied involvement with the book, *Princess in Love*, almost until it was published in October 1994. Yet several weeks earlier Diana, concerned about rumours of his treachery, invited

Hewitt to lunch at Kensington Palace. He was uncharacteristically nervy and evasive. While he dismissed the notion of a book, he did admit that he had always wanted to be a character in a Mills and Boon novel. 'Now he has had his wish,' the princess commented acidly shortly afterwards.

What is remarkable about this tawdry episode is how Diana emerged virtually unscathed. Diana's untouchable quality—in contrast to the Duchess of York and her estranged husband—was tested by further exposures concerning her relationship with Oliver Hoare and the forthcoming court case concerning the 'Peeping-Tom' photographs. The public reacted with weary indifference, a sign that 'royal shock horror' fatigue had set in with a vengeance. Yet on the surface, the story, if believed, published in the *News of the World*, told by Barry Hodge, for ten years chauffeur and self-proclaimed 'right-hand man' to Oliver Hoare, should have seen Diana's stock plummet. He claimed that Hoare and the princess had enjoyed an affair, that Hoare's marriage to his French-born wife Diane had virtually collapsed because of his royal relationship and that Diana was certainly the culprit in the 'phone pest' scandal.

There was more, Hodge claimed that, as a result of his friendship with the princess, Hoare was forced to move out of his £2-million home to a tiny one-bedroomed apartment in Chelsea while his wife Diane took tranquillizers and went for sessions of acupuncture to cope with the stress. According to Hodge, after two months he returned to the family home but not before giving the improbable instruction, which may have been wishful thinking, to make enquiries about a new apartment suitable for himself and Diana. 'All the time the princess was chasing him from pillar to post,' confided Hodge. 'He had to get out. The pressure was driving him potty.'

They met, according to the chauffeur, at the home of Mara Berni, co-owner of San Lorenzo restaurant, in Walton Street and at the Brazilian Embassy in Mount Street where Lucia Flecha de Lima played host. During one secret encounter they had a rendezvous at a Knightsbridge café, while on 23 July 1994 Diana arrived at Hoare's house in floods of tears. In a telling aside which amused those who know her well, he said, 'She is a lovely lady but you can't help but get the idea that her idea of a crisis and most other people's idea of a crisis are very different things.'

While the princess poured scorn on claims of secret meetings, pointing out, for example, that on the day she was supposed to be in tears on Hoare's doorstep she was flying to Spain with Princes William and Harry, the intensity of their conversations on the telephone was not so easy to explain away. 'It was "darling this" and "darling that" and lots of passionate-sounding whispering,' claimed Hodge. 'Sometimes she could phone more than twenty times in a day while we were in the car driving around London. If she only called five or six times we thought of it as a quiet day. The sheer number of calls she made used to wear Mr Hoare down. He'd cringe when the phone went off sometimes. And whenever his wife was in the car he'd carefully pull the plug out just a fraction to break the connection, but make it look like the phone was still turned on.'

While Diana's alleged behaviour was entirely consistent with her history of transitory but obsessive friendships, this telephone relationship was not purely one-sided. It was revealed, thanks to a disaffected telephone operative, who tried to sell his story to the *Sun* newspaper, that Hoare had left the princess a number of messages on her personal pager while he was on a business trip in America. One message stated: 'Longing to hear you and love you madly.' Another said: 'Thinking of you every minute', while a third said, 'Tried and tried to call you whenever possible. So concerned and wish I could help. Thinking of you every minute. Feeling very bad about being so far away. Love you.' A middle-aged man in the middle of a menopausal obsession or proof that here was an unlikely Romeo who had wooed and won a princess? Diana made it clear that he was besotted with her—as many men have been and no doubt will be—and that ever since his 'spineless' behaviour during the 'phone pest' scandal, she had little time for him.

The reasons why this made so little impact in the media and, more importantly, on the public, are twofold. So many skeletons have cascaded from the royal cupboard over the last few years that a few more bones of dubious origin make little difference to a public whose appetite has been well and truly sated. At the same time, the princess in her travails with her husband and his family is perceived as the wronged woman who can now do no wrong. Impervious to scandal, the princess was even able to turn an obvious defeat in to a personal triumph. Ever since Diana announced that she was suing Bryce Taylor, the fitness centre manager who took secret snapshots of her working out at a West London gym, and Mirror Group Newspapers, who published the offending pictures, the media had licked their collective lips in anticipation of the first appearance in court of a member of the royal family since King Edward VII. As the High Court hearing, scheduled for February 1995, drew ever closer the princess showed absolutely no sign of backing down, saying that she was prepared to fight, not only for her sake but the future privacy of her children who had to endure of lifetime of attention. Diana told friends: 'I am only interested in justice. It's not a question of money, but I feel very strongly about this. I want to put a stop to this gross invasion of privacy.' Her preparation was such that she had even chosen the outfits for her appearances in court.

Yet behind the show of bravado there was little appetite for the fight among Diana's legal camp. As soon as it became known that Bryce Taylor had won legal aid to help him fund the case, they realized that he had absolutely nothing to lose. Taylor, his legal expenses now underwritten by the taxpayer, lost no time in hiring Geoffrey Robertson QC. As a vociferous and articulate republican, Robertson was relishing the prospect of cross-examining the princess about her knowledge of the photographs and as well as her symbiotic relationship with the media. Her advisers realized that while the princess may win the case she may well lose her reputation. At the same time Mirror Group Newspapers were eager to distance themselves from any possible royal humiliation and on several occasions had been close to settling the case out of court.

With Bryce Taylor about to fly from his home in Auckland, New Zealand, for London's High Court, royal lawyers and newspaper executives went in to overdrive. After hours of negotiation they hammered out a deal which was satisfactory to all parties. The princess won a front-page apology from the *Daily Mirror* who also paid all legal costs as well as handing over the offending pictures. In addition a substantial donation, around £30,000, was made to a charity of her choice. Diana, who was on tour in Japan at the time the news was broken, was all smiles when she went walkabout among enthusiastic crowds as delighted courtiers told accompanying journalists, 'Her Royal Highness is pleased that her determined stance was so completely vindicated.'

At first sight it was a total and overwhelming success for the princess. Further examination showed it to be a Pyrrhic victory. Far from leaving the negotiations empty-handed, Bryce Taylor walked away with around £250,000, the lion's share of the money from the sale of the photographs, and ten times the amount paid to Diana's charities. The man who so distressed the princess with his sneaky behaviour that she was persuaded to withdraw from public life was able to prove that grime does pay—and pay handsomely.

While the scandals surrounding the princess merely frayed the edges of her popularity, Prince Charles's decision to allow TV journalist, Jonathan Dimbleby, to write his authorized 'kiss and tell' biography unpicked wholesale the threads of loyalty and affection which bind the tapestry of the British monarchy to its people. Condemned as 'the longest abdication note in history', *The Prince of Wales: A Biography* offended the Queen and the Duke of Edinburgh, upset his children and estranged wife, mortified the Parker Bowles family, while by turns distressing and exasperating his supporters in the Church, Parliament and the media in Britain and abroad. The portrait of Prince Philip as a bullying father and Charles's unhappy schooldays were overshadowed by his candid confession that he had enjoyed three affairs with Camilla Parker Bowles and that he was forced by his father in to marrying a girl he did not love. 'It is the most vindictive royal revenge since Henry VIII cut off Anne Boleyn's head,' commented a member of the Queen's household.

Days before the book appeared, the prince, rather belatedly, acknowledged that the emotional fallout from his book would be severe. He twice telephoned Diana and warned her to 'keep her head down'. In one conversation he told his estranged wife that her eating disorder would be described. Her hackles were raised and she told him firmly: 'I hope you pointed out that it was a symptom, not a cause, of the marriage breakdown.' He also admitted that he was beginning to have doubts about the project and his decision to cooperate so fully with Dimbleby, confessing that it had caused some friction between himself and Commander Richard Aylard, his private secretary who had masterminded the operation. Indeed, such was Aylard's involvement, that days before the book's serialization in the *Sunday Times* in October 1994, he contacted those of Charles's friends who had spoken to Dimbleby and gave them a list of possible press questions and their expected responses.

It was, however, the tearful response of Princes William and Harry which most concerned Diana when she spoke to them on Sunday night during their regular telephone calls from Ludgrove. In spite of all her best efforts to protect them from hurtful headlines, they couldn't help but be aware of the topic that dominated television, radio and newspaper coverage that day. What struck deepest was the tabloid screamer which said: 'Charles: I've never loved Diana.' In fact, Charles had never said that; it was Dimbleby's interpretation from speaking to friends of the prince. No matter: that assertion, together with the claim that Prince Philip had forced their father in to a marriage he was reluctant to undertake, naturally troubled the youngsters. That night, before she went to bed, Diana resolved to visit her sons in Berkshire the next day. While Prince Charles was 400 miles away with the Queen Mother on her estate of Birkhall in Scotland, it was Diana who was left to mollify the young princes.

On the morning of Monday 17 October she arrived at their school and was ushered to the headmaster's study. The boys were subdued but eager to hear their mother's version of events. 'Is it true, mother,' blurted out Prince William, 'is it true that daddy never loved you?' Diana had already anticipated their questions and told them simply: 'When we first married we loved each other as much as we love you both today.' It was an explanation of sorts but disguised the reality of that fateful union. As her one-time astrologer, Penny Thornton, revealed on TV, Diana knew that Charles did not love her even before the wedding. Penny Thornton said: 'Charles categorically stated to her he didn't love her. She knew that full well as she walked down the aisle.'

This admission by Diana's astrologer was but one of a veritable babble of statements from those inside the royal circle who would normally have taken their royal secrets to the grave. The serialization of Charles's book, which overshadowed the Queen's historic tour of Russia, prompted the Duke of Edinburgh to summon a journalist to Windsor Castle to discuss the Russia visit and to emphasize the fact that, as a general rule, members of the royal family did not discuss personal matters. This coded rebuke was matched by an openly hostile verdict from Prince Charles's cousin, Marina Mowatt, the daughter of Princess Alexandra. 'He doesn't express any remorse for straying from his marital vows, no apologies to his family, his kids, even his wife,' she complained. 'I just couldn't shrug off the feeling that the documentary and the book were all part of Charles's concern for his popularity rating more than any genuine concern for real people.' She also condemned its 'unfair' portrayal of Diana as a 'neurotic' woman. 'She comes across as a pretty desperate and powerless woman and there's hardly a mention of her sense of fun and humour or any of her good points.'

The Parker Bowleses broke their traditional silence and spoke candidly and angrily about Charles's behaviour. Camilla's then in-laws, Simon and Carolyn Parker Bowles, described the prince as 'very mixed-up' and 'hurtful' who had 'dumped Camilla in a heap' by admitting their affair. Simon said, 'Prince Charles does not have our sympathy at the moment. You can't go back and blame your upbringing on your parents as he has done.' Andrew Parker Bowles's younger brother Richard was more forthright. 'I have to wonder if Charles is fit to be king,' he said. 'Charles has compromised my eldest brother and with it the family name. He has betrayed one of his most loyal subjects. What he did was inexcusable, to take his problems and air them in public. I question his sanity. He was ill-advised and self-centred to the point of arrogance. The whole thing was unnecessary and deeply shaming.' Perhaps the most eloquent and saddest footnote of all came two months later when, after twenty-one years of marriage, Camilla and Andrew Parker Bowles decided to divorce. 'I cannot go on living someone else's life,' the publicly cuckolded brigadier told a friend.

If the emotional fallout was painful, the effect on

the institution of monarchy was profound. In an opinion poll, a third of Anglican vicars believed that Charles and Diana should divorce as soon as possible and half opposed Charles remarrying in church. Even more worrying for the Crown was the news that forty per cent of backbench MPs said they wanted the monarchy replaced in the future. Prince Charles's behaviour had his supporters wringing their hands in alarm. The conservative commentator Charles Moore, a staunch supporter of the prince, noted that Charles had spurned the entire system which was designed to protect him, while another ally who helped in the initial stages of the Dimbleby book said, 'I want a king I can respect not a man that I pity.' Simon Jenkins, former editor of *The Times*, was more direct. 'The prince's latest act of public introspection certainly suggests an unsound mind,' he wrote. Various opinion polls showed rapidly declining respect for the monarchy, the majority of the British public believing that the institution no longer gave value for money. Even diehard loyalists had lost confidence in the future defender of the faith. A poll of *Majesty* magazine readers condemned Prince Charles as 'emotionally weak, demanding and indecisive' and as having caused the 'greatest harm to the monarchy'. Nearly two thirds believed his standing could never be fully restored following revelations of his affair, while more than half said he shouldn't be crowned if he remarried. The Queen's former private secretary, Lord Charteris of Amisfield, candidly admitted, 'The Queen is enough of a realist to know there is nothing for it but to sit it out. She believes the monarchy is strong enough to withstand change and analysis.'

It was going to be a long wait as the prince's book, rather than stem the tide of speculation about his life, merely provoked a flood of tawdry reminiscences from royal staff who believed that, as the prince had made money for charity by selling his story, they should cash in too. Many of the revelations served to flesh out details of the secret affair of the prince and Mrs Parker Bowles which they had enjoyed for most of their adult lives. One former employee recalled how Charles was nicknamed the 'Prince of Darkness' because he always arrived and left Middlewick House, Camilla's home, in the middle of the night. There were descriptions of Camilla's bedroom even down to the fact that when the prince came to stay two wine glasses were left by the bedside in the morning.

The prince's valet Ken Stronach was even more specific. He claimed that he scrubbed the grass stains off Charles's pyjamas after he and Camilla had dallied in her garden, while his sneaked photograph of Charles's bedside table at Highgrove showed a picture of Camilla outside Birkhall, the Queen Mother's Scottish home. For his betrayal, Stronach was sacked, his ignominy complete when he lost his job as a security guard at Battersea power station when his daughter Tracy told the world that her father had sexually abused her for ten years.

This procession of graphic, at times sordid, disclosures once again renewed the debate about Charles's fitness to be king, a debate which has simmered since 1992. His biography served to re-focus attention on the seductive notion that the nation should simply skip a generation and make William the next monarch. While this is an essentially sterile debate—an hereditary monarchy is just that—it brings in to sharp relief the tug of war between the Prince and Princess of Wales for the heart and mind of the future king. In fact, Diana believes that Charles will never become king and that, even if he does ascend the throne, albeit as a lame-duck sovereign, he is likely to be drawing his pension if the Queen lives as long as the Queen Mother. It means that, like Edward VII, his reign will be relatively brief and that the flag bearer for the monarchy in the next century will be Prince William. So the manner of his grooming is vital.

As a result, the princess, whatever her vacillations about her own future, has invested much of her ambition in her sons, particularly William. Over the years she has emphasized her determination to bring up her children in a very different manner from that of previous royal generations. She believes that the constricted royal upbringing has left members of the royal family emotionally stunted and unable or unwilling to understand the day-to-day realities of a modern, multi-cultural society. The furore about Charles's miserable schooldays revealed in his biography reinforced her convictions. As she told friends, 'He can't go on forever blaming everything on me, his parents or his unhappy childhood.' Her visits with the princes to society's underprivileged as well as her willingness to let her sons lead a reasonably normal life, wearing, for example, trendy American-style casual clothes, rather than the tweeds and ties preferred by her estranged husband, are an intrinsic part of her philosophy. As she told a friend, 'I want them to experience what most people already know—that they are growing up in a multi-racial society in which not everyone is rich, has four holidays a year, speaks standard English and has a Range Rover.'

Her common-sense approach, attempting to groom the future sovereign to be in step with the mood of the nation, is strangely at odds with the direction in which William is now moving. So determined to avoid the misfortunes of her own upbringing, Diana now sees her life mirroring that of her parents, the late Earl Spencer and Frances Shand Kydd. It is hard to escape the conclusion that William and Harry will in turn suffer psychologically and emotionally from their parents' separation. Her parents divorced in public acrimony which split the Spencer family for ever and lead to an unbridgeable distance between parents and children. Diana saw the way her mother gradually distanced herself first from her family, then Norfolk society, until finally she went in to self-imposed 'exile' on a Scottish island. Now the princess too is following a similar route, consciously or unconsciously cutting the ties that bind her, emotionally and physically, to her background and aristocratic roots. Her love affair with America is seen by many in her circle as part of that process.

At the same time, as Diana became emotionally

independent of her parents, so the princess today can see her sons growing away from her and not necessarily in her image. Those who have watched the boys mature have remarkably similar perceptions of their characters and development. Since the separation they have seen William become a much more studious, distant and very serious young man; a youngster aware of the debate about his future and much troubled and perplexed by the weight of responsibility it will impose. He has the Windsor stance, the Windsor temper and the Windsor manners. 'He acts a lot older than his years and these days I can see his father in him. It didn't use to be the case,' commented one who has known William since he was a toddler. They see him now protecting his mother rather than needing her protection. Crucially, he is spending less time with her, often spending weekends with schoolfriends at their homes. Last summer, for example, he flew to Corfu and to a cowboy ranch in Montana where he stayed with schoolchums.

At the same time, as many mothers have discovered, William and his brother are now at an age where the princess' visits to watch them play games are socially embarrassing. The royal soon-to-be teenager is no longer as enamoured with the ersatz thrills of Thorpe Park amusement park as in earlier days. Instead, he loves the country pursuits that his father so enjoys. Recently he went on his first 'grownup' shooting party with a group of schoolfriends. He even took along his own part-time valet, Clive Allen, a former chauffeur to Prince Charles. Last summer the prince taught his boys the art of fly fishing by the banks of the river Dee in Balmoral—naturally Harry excelled—and has taken them 'cubbing'—hunting fox cubs with the Beaufort Hunt. Charles has even hired the renowned huntsman, Tom Normington, to teach the boys the finer arts of this controversial field sport.

In September 1995, the prince starts at his senior school, Eton, the *alma mater* to the British Establishment. It is a school of academic excellence, sporting achievement and effortless privilege, an establishment that grooms future prime ministers as well as pupils so wealthy that they have been known to burn piles of £5 notes for fun. Rightly or wrongly, it stands as a symbol of Britain's enduring class system and it will cost the taxpayer around £2 million to pay for William's security during his five-year tenure—£85,000 has been spent already on a high-powered Range Rover fitted with surveillance equipment.

While both parents discussed the choice of school, it is noticeable that Prince Charles's links to the establishment are much more firmly rooted. When he was at Gordonstoun he was tutored by Dr Eric Anderson, who passed on a love of Shakespeare. Anderson subsequently became headmaster of Eton and, in later life, the prince regularly visited him there where he enjoyed reading aloud from Shakespeare. It was Dr Anderson, a regular visitor to Highgrove, who was the guiding hand behind the Prince of Wales's Shakespeare school. Again, the choice of Manor House and William's housemaster,

Dr Andrew Gailey, was largely at Dr Anderson's recommendation.

As William moves in to his father's orbit, the princess' protestations that she wants to break with the past as far as the upbringing of her children is concerned have a peculiarly hollow ring. At thirteen, William has his own valet, bodyguards, a passion for hunting, shooting and fishing and a place at a school that is a byword for elitism. If Queen Victoria were alive today she would entirely approve of William's progress, so that, far from being a flag bearer for a new-style monarchy, Prince William is more likely to be a junior version of his father. His life merely mirrors the day-to-day world of the Windsors, an existence of assumed advantage and privilege, where, to pluck a few examples at random, Prince Charles thinks nothing of using the royal flight to carry his home-grown vegetables from Highgrove to Scotland, or dispatching his valet to London to pick up his favourite gardening boots—a pair of desert boots so worn that they are held together with insulating tape—or carrying his wooden Victorian toilet seat to be installed wherever he is staying. A life where, when the Prince of Wales stays at Craigowan on the Queen's Scottish estate, he expects, nay demands, his bathroom to be painted pink—his preferred colour— and deems it only right and proper that it is repainted blue when the Duke of Edinburgh visits.

As the monarchy rapidly freefalls in to an irrelevant sideshow, particularly abroad, does the lifestyle and coaching of Prince William really matter? The scandals of the last few years have fatally damaged the moral authority of the royal family so that, while they are still keen to lecture the public on how they should live their lives, society has largely turned a deaf ear to their nostrums. It is remarkable just how quickly reverence has turned to ridicule; architect Will Allsop, for example, suggesting that Buckingham Palace be converted in to a casino, and the Charles and Diana debacle turned in to a West End musical.

At the same time, the republican debate, so widely ventilated over recent years, has a tired air, largely because high on the list of suggested presidents are members of the royal family themselves, particularly Princess Anne. More dangerous than any latter-day Tom Paines are Brussels' mandarins. Constitutionally, the European Union continually compromises the Sovereign's position. In the last few months there has been the spectacle of the Chancellor of the Exchequer having to argue, without being assured of success, that the Queen's head should be on any common European currency. Again, during the fishing dispute between Spain and Canada, the prospect of the Queen having to endorse economic sanctions against a country where she is head of state loomed large.

With the possibility of the monarchy being rapidly eroded by the remorseless tide of European history, maybe the modernizing instincts of the Princess of Wales would have had little effect on her son's destiny. Politically sidelined, her personal life rudderless and her ambitions thwarted, the princess can only watch as her sons are moulded to the monarchy an institution blithely unperturbed by the public's antipathy towards its sporting pursuits, its privileges and excesses, or indeed the popularity of the Princess of Wales. When Prince Charles lived at Kensington Palace he had a picture of himself and his father on his desk with the inscription underneath that read: 'I was not born to follow in my father's footsteps.' It seems that, whatever Diana's feelings, William is.

APPENDIX

Arriving at Settlement Terms Should Charles and Diana Divorce

The first meeting

When a client initially consults a solicitor for advice on the breakdown of marriage, it is necessary to try and establish what the client's objectives are. It may be premature to consider a divorce; all aspects need to be taken into account, including the possibility of a reconciliation.

For experienced family lawyers and particularly those who operate under the Code of Conduct of the Solicitors' Family Law Association, the general aim is to promote the sensitive, efficient and economic handling of family disputes and to assist individuals to reconcile their differences and to seek solutions fair to all members of the family and to children in particular.

Separation

The parties can agree to live apart and to draw up a legally enforceable document to record both the actual separation and also the practicalities that flow from the separation. The document usually deals with the children, housing and finance. It may also try and set out the terms upon which the parties will eventually divorce. It does not have the finality of a divorce settlement and within certain parameters can be set aside by the court when the court is asked to consider the family finances in the context of a divorce.

A more formal option is for the parties to decide upon a judicial separation. This is very like a divorce and involves a similar procedure with a petition being served based on the same grounds as for a divorce. It does not end the marriage but simply the requirement for the parties to cohabit; therefore neither party can remarry after this decree of judicial separation has been obtained. This option is rarely used nowadays but is still useful for the client who has strong religious scruples regarding a divorce, but would nevertheless wish the court to deal with both capital and income matters in a similar way as if there had been a divorce.

It is possible for an application to be made to the magistrates' court for a separation. However, because of the reduced powers of the magistrates' court, these applications are usually restricted to low income cases.

When the Prince and Princess of Wales separated formally, they may have entered into a deed of separation. Nevertheless, in view of the complicated nature of each of their public and financial positions, such a document would be both lengthy and complicated, and would probably involve long and tortuous negotiations. It is therefore unlikely that such a document could have been completed in the timescale available before the parties separated. It is more probable that the respective legal advisers concentrated on considering the future implications of the separation and, in particular, the possibility of a divorce with all its attendant problems.

Divorce

The English divorce system is still based on 'fault'. It is necessary to show that the marriage has irretrievably broken down. The court will require the breakdown to be illustrated by one of five factors:

1. Adultery
2. Unreasonable behaviour (This can include all types of behaviour whereby a spouse cannot reasonably be expected to live with the other party. It can include an improper association with another person whether or not adultery can be proved.)
3. Desertion, provided it is in excess of two years

4. Living apart and consent, provided it is for two years and the person who is not taking the proceedings consents to the divorce. This is generally referred to as the 'friendly divorce'

5. Living apart for five years. In these circumstances a divorce can be obtained even if the other party does not consent. It is nevertheless possible to ask the court not to complete the divorce until the financial claims have been resolved. This is often a situation where the husband is the petitioner and the wife is concerned to stop the final decree until her financial claims have been settled to her satisfaction. The final decree allows a husband to remarry and take on new responsibilities that would tend to reduce his available financial resources for his ex-wife and children.

The Procedure

The petition for divorce is prepared by the lawyer acting for the party who wishes to obtain the divorce. It is necessary for the petition to set out the very basic history of the marriage and it asks for a divorce on the ground of irretrievable breakdown on the basis of one or other of the five factors.

Together with the petition, a document called a statement of arrangements is prepared concerning the children of the family, including what the future proposals are for them; where and with whom they are to live; how they will be supported financially; what contact there will be between the children and each party. It is preferable to agree this document in advance with the other spouse. Even if the proposals cannot be agreed, the form is completed and filed and the other party will have an opportunity of filing a document in reply.

When the divorce petition is served it can either be served by hand or, more usually, by post. The party receiving the petition must decide how to respond. He or she will receive the petition and the statement of arrangements together with a document called a notice of proceedings, which includes an acknowledgement of service. This latter document asks a number of simple, but important questions. For a divorce based on two years' separation it will ask: 'Do you consent to a decree being granted?' For a petition based on adultery it will ask: 'Do you admit the adultery alleged in the petition?' If the allegations in the petition are accepted, the form is returned to the court with the appropriate answers and the divorce will proceed as an undefended suit. In these circumstances, at the next stage the court will consider the documentation. If satisfied, it will allow the divorce to proceed to the pronouncement of decree nisi in open court. It is not necessary for either party to attend the court for this purpose. The judge on the appropriate day will grant a decree nisi and six weeks thereafter the petitioner can apply to make the decree absolute. When this document is received it will finally terminate the marriage.

If the grounds in the petition are not accepted by the other party then the suit will become defended. The court will fix a day for the hearing, which will take place in public. The petitioner will have to attend court and try to prove the allegations obtained in the petition in order to be entitled to the decree nisi. Obviously, in the case of a petition based on two years' separation, if the other party does not consent, that is an end of the matter. In all other cases, it may be possible for the petitioner to prove the grounds contained in the petition despite the denials of the other side.

If the Prince and Princess of Wales decide to obtain a divorce they will have a number of options available.

In December 1994, when they will have been living apart for two years, either of them could file a petition based on two years' separation provided the other party consents. The Princess of Wales could file a petition based on the factor of alleged adultery of Prince Charles in the recent television documentary. It is no longer necessary for the princess to name the co-respondent; the court rules make it optional whether the allegation of adultery is made with a named party or not.

Would there be any benefit for the Princess of Wales to sue for divorce on the grounds of adultery? It would not affect the ultimate financial settlement. The court does not take into account conduct in assessing financial claims unless it would be inequitable to disregard it. Adultery would not usually come within that definition. It does nevertheless remain a bargaining lever. Prince Charles would obviously wish the divorce to proceed with the minimum amount of publicity, and any allegations of adultery would obviously fuel the tabloid press. If there is to be a divorce, he would almost certainly prefer it to be based on two years' separation with consent.

Perhaps the most important element of the divorce will be the position of Prince William as heir presumptive. I have explained that when a petition is issued a statement of arrangements is also lodged with the court setting out the arrangements for the children. I anticipate that the information on this form will be kept to a minimum as the parties are unlikely to want the detailed arrangements regarding the children to be lodged at court. I therefore anticipate there will be a separate private document, which will deal with these arrangements.

Since The Children Act 1989, the court no longer uses the emotive terms of custody and access. Instead it refers to residence and contact. The Princess of Wales will wish to protect her position as mother of the boys, and will want to make sure that they spend as much time with her as possible. Prince Charles will probably have a similar agenda. The situation is complicated by Prince William being heir presumptive. The advisers will therefore need to consider his special position. The advisers to Prince Charles will be concerned as to what would happen should the Princess of Wales decide to live abroad or remarry. Both courses would also affect the financial situation. There will also be practical problems, eg, how much of the school holidays are to be spent with each parent, and whether the children should always spend Christmas with the Queen and the royal family at Sandringham.

If agreement regarding the children is not possible, the ultimate sanction is to ask the court to decide any of the outstanding issues. This is the last course the advisers would want. Both William who is twelve and Harry who is ten will be of an age when a judge deciding such an issue would probably take into account the wishes of the boys themselves. It would therefore involve the embarrassment of the children being required to attend court 'in camera', where a judge would make a decision on the matters in dispute.

There is also an interesting additional problem in relation to the princes. Regardless of what the Prince and Princess of Wales may want in respect of the children, the Queen has at common law an absolute right and authority for the care and education of the two boys and, in particular, in respect of the heir presumptive. This right was last recognized in 1772 and the law has not been altered since then. In theory, at least, the Queen could therefore override the wishes of the parents and insist on where and how the children are to be educated, and with whom and by whom they are to be brought up.

Financial Settlement

In any financial settlement the objective will be to obtain a reasonable division of the assets and income so that the needs and responsibilities of the husband, wife and the children can be met.

Initially, this is achieved by both parties revealing their assets and income to each other's lawyers. They are under a duty to the court to be completely honest and to make a full and frank disclosure. If the exercise is approached on a sensible basis each provides a schedule of their assets and liabilities so that the lawyers can assess what would be a reasonable division. If the parties are unable to reach agreement, an application is made to the court and in that application both parties will file sworn statements (affidavits) setting out the same financial details, and asking the court to make an appropriate order.

Usually the wife is the party making this application on the basis that she requires financial support and security for herself and any children. The application is heard by a district judge in chambers, when both parties, represented by their solicitors, or more likely barristers, will usually be ordered to attend, for cross-examination. Members of the public are not allowed in to this hearing and the matter is conducted by the judge on a relatively informal basis. The judge will then decide what he considers is fair and reasonable in all the circumstances.

What is reasonable?

An order that will achieve, in as far as possible, financial independence taking into account various statutory factors.

What would a divorce solicitor want to know?

1. The children's reasonable needs, including the special needs of the heir to the throne

2. Whether or not the Prince and Princess of Wales entered into a marriage settlement? If so, what did it include? Did it include provision for what might happen in the event of a divorce? Was the Princess of Wales given any opportunity for independent legal advice before signing such a document or was she presented with a fait accompli? Prenuptial agreements are not legally binding.

3. What are the financial resources of Prince Charles, both in his own right and also by reason of his interest in the Duchy of Cornwall?

4. What are the financial circumstances of the Princess of Wales?

5. What are her reasonable needs for the future?

6. Would a divorce mean an end of her public life?

7. Consideration of the Princess of Wales's housing requirements and reasonable security needs for herself and the children

8. Consideration of the gifts that have been made during the marriage and, in particular, to what extent they are personal or gifts made to the state

9. The possibility of inheritance and whether either party has any interests in any settlements

What is known, or reasonably can be guessed?

Prince Charles is entitled to the income from the Duchy of Cornwall but only until he ascends the throne. He has no claim to the capital. The accounts of the Duchy of Cornwall suggest that the assets of the duchy exceed £90 million and the net income is approximately £4 million. Prince Charles has indicated that he will start formally to pay income tax at 40% on his income, although he will offset any expenses incurred on public duties. It was also recently reported that the Duchy of Cornwall purchased Highgrove from the prince for the sum of £3 million; therefore he should have at least this amount available as his personal wealth. It has to be assumed that he has other private wealth, which he has accumulated over the years from the income that he has received from the Duchy of Cornwall and from other sources. It is also relevant to mention that when he ascends the throne his financial position will alter radically and he will become one of the richest men in the world. There is no inheritance tax payable on assets passing to the next sovereign and therefore the Queen would be less likely to pass assets to Prince Charles during her lifetime.

The Princess of Wales

There is little information regarding her wealth. It was reported that the princess received approximately £100,000 when she sold her flat in Coleherne Court shortly after her marriage. She is also a discretionary beneficiary under the terms of her father's will. There have been estimates in respect of her jewellery, which have valued it at approximately £20 million. The ownership of this jewellery is a matter of debate, in particular whether the jewellery itself was given to the Princess of Wales personally, or whether it consists of gifts to the state for which she is effectively trustee. All the princess's expenses are presently met by Prince Charles from his income from the Duchy of Cornwall; she lives in a grace-and-favour home at Kensington Palace by courtesy of the Queen.

How would the court approach the Princess of Wales's claims?

The Matrimonial Causes Act 1973 stipulates the matters that the court must have regard to before reaching any decision. The first consideration is the welfare of any minor children of the family who have not attained the age of eighteen. The court would therefore need to look at the position of both Princes William and Harry to satisfy itself that, in any settlement, the arrangements were suitable for the children. The court would therefore be considering the position regarding the children and in particular the position of the heir presumptive. Some of the other matters that the court is required by law to consider are as follows:

1. The income, earning capacity, property and other financial resources of both parties, together

with any reasonable increase in the earning capacity of either party that can be expected

2. The financial needs, obligations and responsibilities, which each of the parties to the marriage has, or is likely to have, in the foreseeable future

3. The standard of living enjoyed by the family before the breakdown of the marriage.

It is interesting to reflect that the law changed in 1984. Before that date the court was required to put the claimant as far as possible into the position he or she would have been in but for the divorce. This would have been a much higher obligation and would have meant that the court was under a duty to try and maintain the Princess of Wales's standard of living, whereas now it is only required to have regard to her standard of living before the separation and may then, for example, decide it was too high.

The court is also required to consider the age of the parties and the duration of the marriage, and the conduct of each of the parties if that conduct is such that it would, in the opinion of the court, be inequitable to disregard it. It has been explained earlier that conduct has to be gross in order to affect a financial settlement and there is nothing to suggest in either the conduct of the Prince of Wales or the Princess of Wales that conduct would be relevant. The court is also required to consider whether or not there should be a clean break between the parties whether now or in the future.

Taking all these matters into account, the Princess of Wales obviously has a very substantial claim which, to a large extent, will be based on her reasonable needs. These could be met by:

(a) A capital payment to cover the purchase of a house or houses and for the balance of the capital to be invested to provide maintenance for the princess plus reasonable financial support for the children

or

(b) a capital payment (not as large as in (a)) to cover the cost of the purchase of a property and to provide a financial cushion, together with maintenance, for the princess and reasonable financial support for the children

(c) the least attractive position for the princess would be the provision of a grace-and-favour home plus maintenance, and financial support for the children.

The court is required to consider a clean break and where the assets are reasonably substantial, the court will always move in this direction in an attempt to separate completely the finances of the two parties to minimize any future conflict. Is it possible therefore to provide a capital sum which would meet the requirements of (a) above? In other words to provide a house or houses for the princess and leave sufficien capital which would then produce income which would enable the princess to enjoy a reasonable standard of living. The court in assessing the amount of capital that would be payable would not be seeking to provide the Princess of Wales with such a large sum that it would enable her to live off the income leaving the capital to pass on to her beneficiaries on her death. It would be looking at providing a smaller capital sum so that by the time she dies the capital fund would be exhausted. The courts do sometimes use a calculation called a Duxbury Calculation, where the assets are substantial, for assessing the value of this capital fund. This is not an exact science and each case is dependent on its own special circumstances. Nevertheless, an example would be that a wife of forty-two, who was entitled to expect an annual income of £100,000, could expect a capital fund in excess of £2 million. This would be based on a life expectancy of thirty-nine years. The court would not normally be looking at this type of settlement for someone as young as the Princess of Wales. Usually, the court would say that someone of her age ought to be able to support herself or assist in supporting herself in the future, once the children are no longer dependent upon her. There are obviously many reasons for saying that this is not an appropriate argument in the Princess of Wales's case, and I am sure that her advisers will be pressing for the largest capital payment possible. The court would also consider the question of the princess's jewellery and whether it should be brought into account, together with her discretionary interest in her father's estate.

It has been reported that the Princess of Wales has been looking at London properties between £2 million and £5 million. This is on the basis that the property would need to be reasonably large to provide for her staff and also to give reasonable privacy and security for her and the children. However, although the assets of the Duchy of Cornwall are in excess of £90 million, Prince Charles does not have any right to this capital, and the court would therefore not be able to force Prince Charles to pay any of that money to the Princess of Wales. Her capital claims could only be based on the capital wealth of Prince Charles and although we know he has £3 million following the sale of Highgrove, it is uncertain how much more wealth he does have. Nevertheless, because of the almost certainty that he will inherit the majority of his mother's wealth when he becomes king, the court may be prepared to give to the princess virtually all of the capital in Prince Charles's name.

Prince Charles does, however, receive a substantial annual income and therefore his advisers would probably argue that any settlement would have to be based on a relatively small capital sum, together with a maintenance settlement, which will continue during the princess's life or until remarriage. From the Princess of Wales's point of view, because maintenance is always variable, she would know that if her circumstances changed there could be a possibility of the maintenance being reduced or ceasing if she remarried.

The assessment of the maintenance would be based on Prince Charles's income which, after making allowance for tax, would be at least £3 million per year. A wife's maintenance claims usually amount to about a third of the husband's net income provided she has no income of her own. Prince Charles does not receive an allowance from the civil list and therefore his advisers will wish to reduce the net income by the cost of his public duties. These have been estimated by royal observers at a minimum of £1 million although part of that figure may include some of the Princess of Wales's expenses. Deducting both income tax and a notional figure of £1 million for public duties leaves an approximate net income of £2 million. Therefore on the one-third basis the Princess of Wales would have a claim for maintenance of about £660,000. The court would also seek to establish what her reasonable needs were, and if they were less than one-third of his net income, then her claim could reduce.

It is difficult to assess the Princess of Wales's needs. Prince Charles has indicated that he spends £160,000 a year on her 'grooming'. Adding to this the cost of running her household will obviously produce a large figure, although the cost of her household will depend very much on her public duties and also how many properties are involved. Her advisers will try and maximize this while Prince Charles's advisers will seek to show that her budget is too high and needs to be reduced. It is difficult to see how an annual figure greater than £500,000 net could be justified.

Prince Charles, and to some extent the royal family, in particular the Queen, would also need to take into account the particular situation of the Princess of Wales and the need for her to be seen to be able to enjoy a reasonable standard of living appropriate for the mother of the heir to the throne. It may therefore be necessary for the Queen to consider assisting Prince Charles by providing sufficient capital to enable a settlement to take place. The Queen may be prepared to consider creating a settlement, whereby the princess would have a life interest in a fund which could provide a property for her with the proviso that the fund would revert to her children on her remarriage or decease. Without the help of his mother, Prince Charles does not appear to have the capital available to satisfy the princess's needs and to effect a clean break.

The financial negotiations inevitably will remain secret, and it is most unlikely that the court will be asked to resolve the Princess of Wales's financial claims. Publicity will nevertheless be an interesting and possibly an important issue. As long as the princess can maintain the goodwill of the public, she is in a strong bargaining position. Should the public perception of her change, this may have a direct and damaging effect on the value of her claims.

* * *

To summarize, in the financial negotiations, the Princess of Wales is vulnerable because of:

1. Her wish to retain her influence with the children and, in particular, an unfettered right to bring up the children
2. Her probable wish to retain a respected public image and possibly some public life and recognition as mother of the heir to the throne
3. A need/wish to maintain an expensive lifestyle independent of the royal family.

Her major advantages are that:

1. She could decide to petition Prince Charles on the grounds of adultery and fight him in the courts for a financial settlement
2. If she sits back and does nothing there is a possibility that she will one day be Queen
3. She could threaten to sell her jewellery because her financial needs were not being met. This would possibly produce unpleasant publicity for Prince Charles, provided her requirements were not seen as outrageous.

Prince Charles's major advantages are:

1. Apparently he does not have access to any large capital wealth and therefore would not be able to meet a massive, 'once and for all' settlement

2. On his mother's death he will become one of the richest men in the world and is therefore probably in a situation where he can persuade his mother to assist a financial settlement to provide the type of settlement that would be acceptable to the Princess of Wales.

Prince Charles is vulnerable because:

1. Constitutionally, his advisers will be anxious to resolve the position of the Princess of Wales, before Prince Charles becomes King
2. Naturally, his wish to maintain his influence with the children
3. He will not want to be seen to be mean to the Princess of Wales in any settlement
4. He will wish to limit adverse publicity.

On the basis of achieving a clean break and based on the Princess of Wales's ability to establish a need for an annual net income of at or near £500,000, I would expect that her advisers would be prepared to consider a once-and-for-all settlement in the region of £15 million.

GEOFFREY WATERS
*Divorce Lawyer and Partner
with Wedlake Bell Solicitors*

Index

Index

Index

Index

Index